# LADIES AND GENTLEMEN:
# THE INIMITABLE MEL BROOKS!

Capturing all the wacked-out wit that is his alone, *Mel Brooks—The Irreverent Funnyman* reveals the man behind the merriment and the people who helped make him the master he is today.

From a poor kid growing up in the Williamsburg section of Brooklyn, Mel Brooks has become one of America's zaniest and most creative comics. Here is the incredible tale of how he got there: his early bits on the Borscht Circuit; writing comedy for Sid Caesar's *Show of Shows* in the Golden Days of TV; his hilarious "2000-Year-Old Man" records with Carl Reiner; and finally the impious sell-out movies *Blazing Saddles* and *Young Frankenstein* that have catapulted him to fame as a comic genius.

# MEL BROOKS
## THE IRREVERENT
## FUNNYMAN

### BILL ADLER/JEFFREY FEINMAN

PLAYBOY PRESS

MEL BROOKS—THE IRREVERENT FUNNYMAN

*Front cover illustration by Chuck Slack.*
*Back cover photo by UPI.*

Published simultaneously in the United States and Canada by
Playboy Press, Chicago, Illinois. Printed in the United States of
America. Library of Congress Catalog Card Number: 75-36300.
First edition.

Books are available at quantity discounts for promotional and
industrial use. For further information, write our sales-promotion
agency: Ventura Associates, 40 East 49th Street, New York,
New York 10017.

# Table of Contents

# 1

## The Kaminsky Baby

Kate Kaminsky had four sons. Each, in his Mama's eyes, was a gift from heaven. Irving was the oldest, with a brain like Einstein. Lenny was as good as gold. Bernie was an athlete, and Melvin—well Melvin was the baby. "Melb'n," his Grandma called him.

It was hard times in 1930. The bright future offered immigrants and their children was stolen from Kate Kaminsky. When her youngest child was two years old, Kate's husband died from tuberculosis. Mama was left to bring up four sons alone.

The death of Max Kaminsky was a severe blow which cost the family its small stability in the new world. The baby especially always yearned for the father he never knew. Who was Papa? A Russian Jew from Kiev, Max Kaminsky worked as a process server. He sang in a strong tenor voice and loved to tell jokes. He died young with the promise of his life before him, held out like a gift, then snatched rudely away. That was all Melvin ever knew about Papa. An extinguished light.

But there was still the indomitable Mama.

How did Kate Kaminsky survive? She fought poverty, language barriers, prejudice against foreigners from Americans, anti-Semitism from other immigrants. Desperately, she clung to the center of Jewish life in the Williamsburg section of Brooklyn, one of the hardest ghettos in New York. She battled poverty like a tugboat fighting a high gale at sea. Sinking, rising to the surface, sinking, and rising again. Little by little making headway, delivering her treasure—her four sons who would make their mark in the world.

As the Depression deepened, Jews—especially foreign-born Jews—couldn't get jobs in offices or as skilled labor. Kate Kaminsky, born in Kiev, did the only work she could get—factory work in the knitting mills and sweatshops. At night she brought home piece work. Pennies counted, nickels were riches. The two oldest boys went to work in the mills when they were eleven and twelve. When he was old enough, Lenny joined them.

The Kaminsky family survived the Depression. Better than survived, they prevailed. They were frightened and desperate; they were deprived of the most ordinary necessities. Mama spent many nights worrying how she would guide her family safely through one more day in the rough-and-tumble Williamsburg ghetto. Yet the special strength and optimism that immigrants from all over the world brought with them to America saw her through. She never could have left Russia without it.

The Kaminsky style of dancing with life was ingrained in the family. There was the story of Grandpa Kaminsky's voyage to America. "He got here on the boat," his youngest grandson recalls, "and there was another Kaminsky on the boat, a famous violinist. So they thought my grandfather was the violinist and they booked him for a concert. He went to a music teacher to learn how to play the violin. 'No, no,' he told the teacher, 'I gotta know by Thursday.' "

The people who immigrated to the new land were different from those who stayed home. They were looking for something, and willing to take risks to get it. No matter what circumstances drove them from their homeland—famine, poverty, or persecution—they all had at the core daring and courageous spirits. Far from being downtrodden and beaten by their hard fate, the Kaminskys survived their trials with dignity and joy in their family life.

Immigrant life in the first half of the Twentieth Century is recalled today with nostalgia. The bitterness of the struggle is remembered with pride, seldom with remorse. It was a battle, but a battle you could win. Italians, Irish, Poles, and Jews all could win. The key to winning was education.

While they struggled to put food on the table, Irving, Lenny, and Bernie all went to school. They graduated from high school, which in many immigrant households was considered an ultimate achievement. But for Mama's boys it was only the beginning. All three sons graduated from college. And the baby? What was Melb'n doing while all the work and studying was going on? He was holding the family together.

Years later he remembers that so eager were his brothers and mother to hold him, toss him in the air, and carry him lovingly in their arms, that his feet didn't touch the ground until he was six years old.

He was the youngest, the cutest, the funniest—the last baby Mama would have. The treasure. And baby Melb'n knocked himself out living up to his responsibility as the family laughmaker. If clapping his hands would make Mama smile, then winking at her as she watched him out of the corner of her eye would make her hysterical. He learned to mug before he would walk. Sitting up at the dinner table in his mother's lap he would practice gurgles and making faces with an infant clown's awareness of which antics got the biggest laugh from his circle of attentive admirers. "I always expected to be the King of France," he recalls. "I'm still waiting for my crown."

Melvin was a beautiful baby. The bluest eyes, and the biggest smile. Late at night he would tiptoe over to one of his exhausted brothers whose head was drooping over school books. Baby Melvin would tap him on the arm and smile his angelic smile. Then he would cross his eyes and twist his mouth into an idiotic grin.

Melvin had discovered his greatest asset. When he learned to talk, words completed his repertoire of funny faces, grimaces, burps, and gurgles. Words created new dimensions. Now he could tell jokes! And he had them all ready, waiting for a method of expression. What he did with his eyes, his mouth, and his whole body, now he could do with words. Melvin learned to talk when he was sixteen months old. And they say he's never known a moment's silence since.

During his early childhood, the future King of France seldom left his mother's kitchen. In every

Jewish tenement, the kitchen was the hub of activity. In each three-room cold-water flat there was a front parlor, a lightless center bedroom, and the kitchen. At night the parlor would be converted to a second bedroom. But all family life took place in the kitchen—cooking, school work, and piece work from the factory. Visitors sat in the kitchen and talked in the late evening while Mama sewed. Melvin had been born right on the kitchen table, and for the next six or seven years the kitchen was where he held court—singing, dancing, mugging, juggling, cartwheeling, tickling, and joking. This was his work, his contribution to the family. His gift for laughter brought him so much love and attention from his family that he never wanted to grow up.

Several harsh realities faced Melvin when he first went outside to play in the streets of Williamsburg. The first was quickly learned. There was *your* neighborhood, and then there was everybody else's neighborhood. The Irish, Polish, and Italian kids all had their part of the street. The ghetto appeared to be mixed with nationalities, but the kids knew where all the boundaries were. If a Jewish boy ventured into a gentile section, he risked a beating. This was an easy rule to learn. You stuck to your own. New York's famed melting pot never made its inhabitants homogeneous. Because of the isolation of the Jewish community, Melvin was protected from the hard lessons of prejudice in his early years. Everybody he knew was Jewish.

In Brooklyn, where every other kid was a potential Lou Gehrig, pint-sized Melvin Kaminsky failed to shine as a ballplayer. But every kid was also a wise guy. Jewish boys especially had at least as much respect for verbal speed as for speed in handling a ground ball. And Kaminsky was the uncontested champion of the wisecrack. He was so quick-witted that the older boys accepted him into their gang. Once again he ruled, king of the clowns. He ruled because nothing and no one was safe from his barbed tongue. Early on he learned that he could cut any neighborhood bully down to size simply by mimicking his walk, or imitating the way he talked. At home, Melvin had love and adoration; on the street, Kaminsky had respect.

Like all city kids, Kaminsky and his crowd hung out. Hanging out is an acknowledged art form in New York. Kids collect as if by previous appointment on a neighborhood street corner. They stand around and talk. Corner *schtick*, the Jewish kids called it. Italian, Irish, and black gangs hung out too. But there was more sophistication in the brash, cutting dialogues of the Jewish kids. More than any other group, these youngsters were from homes that traditionally respected and cultivated the written and spoken word.

Corner *schtick* was often violent and ugly. Its technique was to make something horrible seem funny. And there were many horrible events occurring daily on the streets of Williamsburg to tax the inventive brain of Melvin Kaminsky. Fires, thefts, beatings, and even suicides. Mel's hiccupping and staggering around in imitation of Mrs. Rosenfeld's *shikeh* husband was always worth a good five minutes' hilarity on the corner. After Mr. Rosenfeld fell off the roof and was killed, Mel's swandive to the sidewalk had the other kids hysterical for half an hour.

Kaminsky was a street kid, always running—skinny, wiry, hard as nails with the other guys. On the street he was smart-ass Mel Kaminsky and anyone who messed with him risked a tongue lashing that could leave permanent wounds. But at home in the kitchen he was still his Mama's baby. Spared the hard work his brothers faced before they reached their teens, Kaminsky poured his drive into stickball, punchball, and wild clowning. He would take bodily risks to get a laugh, swinging from fire escapes, dodging traffic. The streets of Williamsburg are narrow, glutted with cars. To play ball there you needed the agility of an alley cat and the nerve of a high-wire artist.

As with other first-generation immigrants, isolation within his own community gave Kaminsky a strong national identity. Kids were identified by nationality. They were "hebes," or "wops," or "micks." The nationalities were distinctly different from one another, and they clung together for survival. Learning who was "us" and who was "them" was often a painful experience. Off their own ground, Jewish boys were runners, not fighters. But the ghetto was their home base. They carved out their own niche for survival and hung on to it. And the ghetto groups spawned a generation of opposites. Out of Little Italy came Fiorello La Guardia as well as Vito Genovese. From Hell's Kitchen there was both "Mad Dog" Coll and Pat O'Brien. And Williamsburg produced not only a healthy proportion of America's comedians, it also produced "Bugsy" Siegel and Murder, Incorporated.

All of the ethnic groups in New York's ghettos were different from "Americans." But while the

Italians and the Irish warred with each other all week, they were together in Church on Sunday. The Jews were just a little more different.

The reports from outside brought Kaminsky conflicting views of just what a Jew was. On the one hand, all Jews were Communists, brewing revolution in every country and plotting to rip up the stability of decent people. On the other hand, Jews were the money changers and lenders; they ran the banks. A Jew was foxy, scheming, and would do anything for a dollar. They were, in fact, the very capitalists that the dirty Reds were scheming to overthrow. Confusion invaded young Kaminsky's mind—confusion followed by the gradual realization that he had encountered anti-Semitism. Whatever people said about the Jews, they never said anything nice.

These were brutal lessons for a boy. Kaminsky grew a thick skin and gave as good as he got. Sometimes better. But he had a secret life. On the street he was a tough, wisecracking daredevil. At home he was still the princeling. Sweet, good natured, funny Melb'n. His Mama's joy and his brothers' delight. Kaminsky knew what Jewish was. It was love. Home was a place you ran to, never away from. A Jew's best friends were his family, and the safest place in the world was at the kitchen table. The best things and the funniest things in the world were Jewish. The time would come later in his life when it would have been easy for Kaminsky to grow away from Jewishness. But when those times came, Kaminsky deliberately reattached himself to his identity. So much so that he tagged himself, cynically and pridefully, "your obedient Jew," as if to say, before anything else, this is what I am. Above all—Jewish, Jewish, Jewish.

This was his life. Stickball, hanging out, hustling pennies for the movies, running scared. Nights he stayed home with his mother and brothers. Saturdays were for movies. Even the poorest kids could scrounge up ten cents for a day-long bout at the movies on Saturday. Scurrying into the darkened Marcy Theater at ten o'clock on Saturday morning, Kaminsky sat all day watching a series of horror flicks, Westerns, short subjects, and cartoons parade across the screen. The theater was a jumping beehive full of kids—booing, laughing, punching, cheering, and stamping their feet. Kaminsky's mother always knew where to find him on Saturdays. By half-past six in the evening she usually would have to walk to the Marcy and drag her unwilling offspring out by the ear.

Unlike his brothers, Kaminsky hated school. Irving, Lenny, and Bernie worked hard during the day and went to college at night. They were tireless in their efforts to get through school. But the adored baby got all the attention by cutting up. If Kaminsky reasoned at all, he thought why be a scholar? The approval he wanted came from the other kids and from his family. A fast line of wise talk, a few outrageous remarks accompanied by a silly face, got him all the approval he needed. Teachers were the enemy anyway. He didn't have to figure this out. It was clear to him that goofing got him what he wanted. Studiousness got him a lot of hard work.

But Kaminsky grew up in an era when corporal punishment was the rule and conformism the desired goal of education. Children of immigrants were expected to be profoundly grateful for the free education they were getting and to display their gratitude with solemn respect and hard work. Teachers were harsh disciplinarians. But raps across the knuckles or a smart slap on the face were a small price to pay for respect from your peers. The more manic Kaminsky was in school, the more admired he was by his classmates. Punishment only fueled his delirium. The more he was slapped around, the more he laughed. The more he laughed, the more the teacher would attempt to knock the nonsense out of him by brute force.

Even so, he had his good points. No one could beat him at declamation. No matter how mundane the subject, Kaminsky read all his essays to the class as if they were Shakespearean soliloquies. Whether it was "My Summer Vacation," or "My Visit to the Hat Factory," Kaminsky made it sound like high drama. Waving his arms, his blue eyes peering meaningfully at his audience, he gave it everything he had. Eccentric, willful, uncontrollable, brilliant—Kaminsky was out of place in his environment.

So out of place that his mother worried that he might never make anything of himself. To insure his future employment, Mama enrolled Melvin in the Haaran High School of Aviation Trades to learn to be an airplane mechanic. Irving, by now a college graduate in chemistry, was outraged. The baby, he told Mama, would be a scholar just like the rest of the brothers. No mechanic school for Melvin. Irving withdrew Kaminsky from aviation school and sent him to Eastern District High School.

* * *

Kaminsky started working the Catskills summers when he was fourteen. He made his debut in one of the small hotels, playing a district attorney in a murder melodrama called *Uncle Harry*. Scared to death the first time in front of a real audience, Kaminsky dropped a glass of ice water which sent shards of glass and spraying water into the audience. There was a gasp and frigid silence. Terrified, the teenager ripped off his older-man disguise and marched to the edge of the stage to announce: "Okay, I'm sorry. But I'm only fourteen years old." The audience howled, and Kaminsky had his first taste of real performing.

Kaminsky's main job during the summer vacation was as a pool *tummler*. A *tummler* was a free-lance comedian. He wasn't the guy who got to do the show in the evening, but the one who came out by the pool in the afternoons and announced that he was The Man of a Thousand Faces. Kaminsky would make one, two, three, even four of his sure-fire laugh-getting faces. No one smiled. "They waited. Jews are patient." They wanted the entire thousand faces, as promised.

His other routine was to walk off the end of the diving board fully dressed and loaded down with suitcases. Anything for a laugh.

To the children of Jewish immigrants, reared on the streets of Brooklyn and the Lower East Side, the Catskill Mountains were paradise. In the city you might live in a fifth floor walkup, but when you took your long-awaited vacation, you were as demanding and as hard to please as the Czar.

The legendary Jewish watering spas in the Catskills such as Grossinger's and the Concord were run by people who understood how important the perfect vacation was to their guests. Owners understood that guests wanted fresh country air, great food, plenty of linens, and fabulous entertainment.

There were a variety of jobs for show business beginners. The afternoon poolside *tummler*, Saturday-night-only jobs in the smaller hotels, band jobs, social jobs, summer stock—always a spot for an ambitious youngster to get experience. And if you were good, there would be another spot to move up into.

One summer Kaminsky got a job playing drums with a hotel orchestra. He wasn't a great drummer even though his teacher had been a neighborhood boy named Buddy Rich. But a job was a job, and the image of himself behind a set of traps gratified his need to be the center of attention. There might be six horn players in an orchestra, but there was only one drummer.

Like his grandfather, Kaminsky had some trouble with mistaken identity. Mel Kaminsky was confused with the well-known cornet player Max Kaminsky. To avoid disappointed hotel managers and sullen bandleaders, Mel adopted his mother's maiden name of Brookman. But Brookman had too many letters to fit on his drum, so he shortened it to Brooks. Thus legends are born. Mel Brooks, drummer.

One evening, Hollywood style, the standup comic got sick and Brooks née Kaminsky leapt at the chance to go on for him. As in his street corner days, he talked about things happening around him. He drew on the lifestyle of the Jewish hotels. He imitated the hotel manager and anyone else his audience might know. In days of standard mother-in-law jokes, Brooks's material was en-

gaging and funny. He wasn't, however, an overnight sensation. The hotel guests, snatching a
brief week in the country after a year's hard labor
in the city, were a tough audience to please. They
wanted the best. At the same time, they were
sympathetic to a kid beating his brains out for a
laugh. "Your show was very nice, Melvin. But
shouldn't you learn a trade?"

Patriotism was at its peak in 1944. For American Jews, particularly, the Second World War was
a fight for the right. Many of the boys in Kaminsky's high school class dropped out in their senior
year to join the service. Kaminsky was as anxious
as his friends to join up, but his brothers made
him hold the line at school. He graduated from
Eastern High in June of 1944, with his future
self proclaimed in the school year book: "Presi-
dent of the United States."

A month later he was in the army. Once again
Kaminsky found himself a stranger in a strange
land. The army sent him to Virginia Military
Institute, which was being used as a basic training
center during the war. "I rode a horse and cut
down sticks with a sabre," he recalls. "I couldn't
believe it, a little Brooklyn Jewish kid on top of a
big red horse." It was getting late in the war, however, and there wasn't much time left for horses
and games. Kaminsky was sent to Fort Sill, Oklahoma, to train as a combat engineer. If Virginia
was alien to him, Oklahoma was downright hostile. Tough and wiry, Kaminsky was a ninety-
pound weakling compared to the all-American
giants in his unit. "They put a pack on my back
and an extra bandoleer and I couldn't move.
Then this big Texan, six feet-three, a redwood

tree . . . he took my pack and rifle and carried my stuff for five miles. It was an incredible experience. I was nothing but bones and skin. I had to wear a towel when I shot the rifle." Always slender, at Fort Sill Kaminsky's weight fell to one hundred fifteen pounds.

There wasn't much to laugh at when Kaminsky's unit was shipped to Europe toward the end of the year. The first stop was a little town in Belgium. In a few days it would go down in history as the site of the Battle of the Bulge. Kaminsky's job was to deactivate land mines ahead of the infantry. The myth of the heroic G.I. eagerly looking forward to a day's battle finds little sympathy with Kaminsky even today. American soldiers on the battle lines between France and Belgium were paralyzed with fear. Kaminsky was scared in the streets of Brooklyn. And he was scared on the German line. But he survived. Tough, wisecracking, indestructible. His fear was so great that he laughed at dying. And he made others laugh with him. After the Battle of the Bulge, the Germans made a propaganda pitch to Kaminsky's outfit via loudspeaker. In return, Kaminsky set up a loudspeaker of his own and entertained the Germans with what must have been to them an incomprehensible rendition of "Toot-Toot-Tootsie," Jolson style.

As he had handled the morale problem in his mother's kitchen, so he jacked up the spirits of the men around him. On the front, his antics were recognized and appreciated. By the end of the war, he made it into the cast of army reviews. These showmen entertained their fellow soldiers in occupied Germany and later at Fort Dix, New Jersey. The army shows were raucous and wild, just the way Kaminsky liked his humor—three guys in drag imitating the Andrews Sisters.

Out of the army in 1947, Kaminsky enrolled in Brooklyn College just as his brothers had before him. But times had changed. After surviving the brutal blood-letting of the Battle of the Bulge, few things in life appealed to Kaminsky. What, after all, was the point of wasting your life doing something you didn't want to do? But that premise led only to more confusion. What *did* he want to do with his life?

# 2

# From Kaminsky to Brooks
# to Caesar

He thought about going to college. He thought
about getting a job. Neither of these pursuits appealed to him. School had never been his strong
point. And what kind of job could he get? Salesman? The only thing he really enjoyed was show
business. But what kind of job could he get in
show business? There's no easy way to get ahead
in show business. Anyone who has ever made it
will tell you how tough it is. Mel's problem was
worse in a sense because he didn't know exactly
what he would do even if he was in the business.
He knew he wasn't a drummer. He was funny,
but he had never done a straight standup comedy
act. He thought about being an actor.

He got a job as a stagehand and part-time actor
in a theater in Red Bank, New Jersey. The small
playhouse specialized in English drawing-room
comedies. Mel threw his abundant energy into the
life of the theater. He was beginning to grow into
a man of complexity. Yet he was a man chained
to his past as a child. Because he was short and
always clowning, people thought of him as a kid.
Mel resented being treated like the village idiot,

yet he couldn't seem to shed his childhood skin. His humor and antics were irrepressible. He wanted to be a man, but maybe not. Only when he was angry was the grownup Mel Brooks revealed.

The leading man of the company was the young Will Jordan, who later achieved fame as a comedian. Jordan recalls how stunned he was one day when Mel lost his temper. The company director, a neurotic Russian with the unlikely name of Percy Montague, had been riding Mel about something. It blew up into a hot argument. Mel marched on stage, waving his arms and yelling, "I will not be the scapegoat." "We were all so surprised," recalls Will Jordan. "Here was this tough little Brooklyn character suddenly turned eloquent. He was brilliant and literate. He had an extraordinary, unexpected command of language. I didn't even know what a scapegoat was."

Brooks had a bitter view of himself during those days. By his own admission he considered himself physically ugly. He compared his appearance to Sammy Glick in *What Makes Sammy Run*. Budd Schulberg called his Sammy character "ferret-faced," and that is how Brooks saw himself. A ferret-faced, running screwball. "But Mel wasn't like Sammy Glick inside," Jordan remembers. "He was warm and funny and gentle. Just the opposite of the real Sammy Glick."

Even then, Mel had a very deep, masculine voice. But he was disturbed because it had a fuzzy quality. He wanted to talk like an announcer and to that end he would practice imitations of voices he admired. Brooks idolized Al Jolson. He loved Jolson so much that he would imitate him without music for an hour or more. One night when the

curtain was late going up on the scheduled play,
Mel and Will came out and did impressions. A
few years later Will Jordan would become nation-
ally famous for creating the classic impression of
Ed Sullivan, but that night he and Brooks were
just practicing their offstage hobby of mimicry.
"Mel did Jolson and I did Bette Davis. God, we
were awful. But we wouldn't get off the stage. We
kept it up for over an hour."

Show business is a struggle, but it is also a lot
of fun if you're young and ambitious. There is a
camaraderie among the children of the theater
that makes hardship a lark. Survival was old hat
to Brooks. He was an expert. And he was doing
something that he loved to do. So when the Red
Bank Theater folded for lack of funds, Mel, Will
Jordan, and Will's cousin John decided to keep
the company going. They each kicked back their
Actors' Equity salaries and rented a small room in
the area. They were so poor that for six months
the three of them slept crosswise on two army
cots. With Mel taking over the vacant director's
spot, the company continued to put on shows. "I
wouldn't say he was a great director then," recalls
Jordan. "But he had a natural instinct for it. He
just very easily took over the company."

It was in those theatrical days in Red Bank
that Brooks first tried writing. His initial attempts
were not comedic, however. The Second World
War and its aftermath had made a strong anti-
fascist out of him. Along with most of the young
theater crowd in those days, he also had mild
Communist leanings. But he was so young and his
association with politics so meager that he was
never caught up in the politicization that would
ruin the careers of many theater people in the

McCarthy years. Nevertheless, his first short stories reflect a concern with political values. They were serious stories, but self-consciously moralistic. Two cats meet in an alley. One cat lives in a big rich house, the other roams the alleys living by its wits. The rich cat says, how can you live like that? The poor cat says he wouldn't give up his independence for all the money in the world.

Mel was intellectually mature, but still had a childlike, nervous manner. He was defiant and pessimistic. No matter what he did he believed life was going to kick him in the head. This brand of fatalism is characteristically Jewish. Mel felt he was a loser, his fast line of talk only covering up a nobody trying to get by. His energy level was always high. He would burst into a room at the crack of dawn singing "Who cares if the sun shines tomorrow . . . who cares if ships sail in Yonkers . . . tomorrow I'm going to commit suicide."

His feeling of being a loser was transmitted to the people who knew him in those days. When Will Jordan began to achieve some success as a comedian in nightclubs, he didn't see much of Brooks anymore. "I was nervous and on my way up," Jordan says. "I wanted to be around people who were positive. Mel just had that quality of failure."

Success in Mel's eyes was not measured in dollars. He was never impressed by the comics who played the Copacabana for two thousand dollars a week. But someone who performed at the elite Blue Angel or the Reuben Blue, spawning ground of such artists as Jonathan Winters and Judy Holliday, was *important*, even though he might earn only two hundred dollars a week. Brooks knew the difference. "He had very sophisticated taste," recalls Jordan. "Even in his jokes he never went for a cliché, never the obvious, even though he might be talking about some ordinary daily event. He always said the unexpected." When Will received his first booking at the Blue Angel, Mel was ecstatic. As far as Brooks was concerned, that was as good as you could get.

Mel tended to think everyone else in show business was better than he was. One of his idols was Don Appel, who later went on to write for Broadway, but in the late Forties he was a social director at the Avon Lodge, one of the Catskills resorts. In between Red Bank chores, Brooks always managed to get back to the Catskills. This nursery school of show business made "Jewish" synonymous with American comedy. There was something in the combination of Yankee optimism and traditional Jewish irony that created a new brand of humor. Brooks believed that comedy was Jewish because a people who have known so much despair must develop superior clowns to help them survive.

For an entertainer, playing the Borscht Belt either made you or broke you. You needed both brilliance and endurance to succeed. Everyone who is anyone in comedy, from Milton Berle to Woody Allen, has done his time in the mountains.

Working the mountains, Mel Brooks met all the performers who would make it to the top during the golden days of television comedy. They were all knocking themselves out and running flat out. They were hard working and crazed with ambition. And yes, they were funny. Night after night, the Jerrys and Howies and Jacks pummeled their audiences for laughs. If a joke didn't work they would change the delivery. They would try it twice, three times, maybe a fourth time if there was any promise. After that, if it still didn't work, it was out.

A standup comic's job is the roughest in the entertainment business. There are only two audience reactions—laughter and silence. Or occasionally, if he's really bad, verbal abuse. These two responses are fed back to the comic immediately during his performance. The comedian has nothing to work with but himself. No songs, no plot, no dances. Only his fast mouth and his brain. It wasn't enough for the material to be good. The comedian's personality had to be appealing. An audience either loves a comic or hates him. There's nothing in between. There's nothing better than a laugh. Nothing worse than silence.

Brooks ran with the rest of them. He urged Don Appel to introduce him to a rising young comic named Sid Caesar. Did anyone recognize this meeting as a milestone in show business history? Perhaps only Mel Brooks himself. From the beginning he admired Caesar. Sid's performing talent was so great that Brooks didn't even think of trying to compete with him.

Sid Caesar began as a musician. He played saxophone in several Catskills orchestras. He had joined the Coast Guard during the war and was playing for a service band. But like Brooks, he couldn't resist any opportunity to be a clown. Caesar's skill wasn't with words—he was notably inarticulate. But he was a superb pantomimist and a good actor.

After his release from the Coast Guard, Sid was gaining a reputation for brilliance as a standup comic. When he met Mel, the two hit it off immediately. From the beginning, the relationship between Brooks and Caesar was one of hero worship. Caesar was the hero and Brooks the worshipper.

Sid Caesar had had an unhappy childhood. He had been the youngest in his family and unlike Brooks, was largely ignored by his hard-working family. As a youth he had been a runt. He was so aggravated by his physical appearance that he worked out in the gym every day until he turned himself into a muscleman. Sid was so strong that he could send a guy flying across the room with one well-directed punch. In his early twenties he was an extraordinarily gifted comedian, but knew very little about himself. He was given to depression and black moods alternating with rational good humor. He sometimes demonstrated an uncontrollable temper. But he could also be generous, peace-loving, and amusing.

Caesar was formal and rigid with strangers. Mel, who would do anything for a laugh, who was as irrepressible and spontaneous as Caesar was rigid, was the perfect sidekick for Sid. Mel Brooks, underneath his rough exterior, was sensitive to the needs of other people. He understood Caesar.

Mel was so impressed by Sid that he gave up all thought of performing himself. Caesar, as far as Brooks was concerned, was the best. As early as 1947 Mel was writing gags for Sid. Few people ever realized how much of Sid Caesar was really Mel Brooks. It's possible that Caesar didn't know himself. Sid was such a natural mimic that he seemed to absorb the personality of other people. Mel's inventiveness was tailor-made for the performing genius of Caesar. From their earliest days together, Brooks understood the nature of Caesar's ability. He needed to create characters for Sid to lose himself in, for Caesar was never so good as when he was someone else. Nevertheless, Brooks always considered himself inferior to Caesar. He saw himself as a little runt who had nothing to offer, but was just lucky enough to be hanging around someone who was really talented.

Sid got his big break when he was tapped for a cameo role in a movie review called *Tars and Spars.* A few months later, television producer Max Liebman cast him in a new television program, *The Admiral Broadway Review.* Sid immediately called Brooks and asked him for some new material. Caesar's success with that first show was unprecedented. Within a year the weekly experimental program, which starred newcomers such as Marge and Gower Champion and Imogene Coca, became the one-and-a-half-hour-long *Your Show of Shows*—starring Sid Caesar.

Sid wanted Brooks hired as part of the permanent staff of *Your Show of Shows*. Liebman refused. When the new show first went on the air in 1949, the staff writers included Mel Tolkin, Lucille Kallen, and surreptitiously, Mel Brooks. At Caesar's insistence, Brooks hung around in the hallways outside the writers' conference room. When they were stuck for a joke, Caesar would stick his head out the door and Brooks would holler out a half dozen jokes off the top of his head. Caesar paid him fifty dollars a week out of his own pocket.

Brooks was Caesar's security blanket. He never failed to supply the oxygen that Caesar lived on. Eventually even Liebman agreed that Brooks was valuable. Mel was put on as a junior staff writer at two hundred and fifty dollars a week. Tolkin, Kallen, and Brooks built the first year's show into television's biggest hit.

Success, however, was no barometer of good will on the Caesar show. The hostile relationship between Brooks and Liebman continued full pitch. Liebman continuously threatened Brooks with dismissal.

All the writers on the show were aggressive show-offs. No one knows even today why Liebman singled out Brooks to detest, but he disliked him enough to confront Caesar time and again on the question of Brooks's employment. Caesar insisted that Brooks was in—or else. With *Your Show of Shows* foremost in the ratings, both producer and star had tremendous power. Liebman, the producer, could write his own ticket at NBC. Caesar felt there was no show without the star and acted accordingly.

While whom you know and who likes you goes a long way in show business, talent occasionally goes even further. Brooks's obvious contribution to the show, plus Caesar's determination to have his own way, forced Liebman to renew his contract. Caesar's tenaciousness was due to personal loyalty, plus the knowledge that his success was built on the wit and creativity of Brooks. Once more, Brooks survived in a deadly situation. Over the next five years, his salary rose to five thousand dollars a week.

Once on the team, Brooks threw all of his tremendous energy into the scripts. Everything he felt, thought, and observed was burned up in a fever of writing which produced eight major sketches a week for ten years. During those years,

Brooks created enough comedy material for twenty-five full-length motion pictures.

Were the staff writers, so dependent on each other for success, one big happy family? Not even on a good day. The creativity of *Your Show of Shows* was based on the most severe kind of competition. There was more backbiting behind the scenes of *Your Show of Shows* than at the Miss America Pageant. It was a big, hostile family with all the kids competing for Caesar's approval.

The writers of the Caesar show were all maniacs. Brooks would do anything for a laugh, even risk his life. There was no fire escapes to dangle from, so one day he threw himself out of a window and clung to the ledge until he got a laugh from the other writers. He was forever being patched up for scrapes and bruises garnered while jumping on the furniture, turning handstands which collapsed in mid-air, or banging his head against the wall.

Today, Caesar's roster of *Your Show of Shows* writers looks like a list of Who's Who in Comedy. The original trio of Brooks, Kallen, and Tolkin was joined by Joe Stein, who later would write *Fiddler on the Roof*, and Larry Gelbart, of *M*A*S*H* renown. Then there were the Simon boys, Neil and Danny, who graduated to become princes of New York and Hollywood, respectively. Even the clerical help was brilliant. Mike Stewart quit typing for the group to write *Hello Dolly!* and *Bye, Bye Birdie*. He was replaced by a skinny, wiry-haired kid named Woody Allen.

If Mel and the other writers were crazy, Caesar was stark, raving mad. Suddenly catapulted to national fame as few comics had ever been before, he responded badly to the formidable pressure. At the top of the world at twenty-seven years old, Caesar was given to depressed moods which alternated with temper tantrums. When he didn't like a sketch, he would storm into the writer's room, lift a large metal desk off the floor, and slam it into the wall. Youngsters like Woody Allen cowered. Brooks, perched on top of a filing cabinet, would jump Caesar from behind, pleading "Down, boy." Only Brooks could make Caesar laugh on days like those. He was the traditional jester to the king. While Brooks was pathetically subservient to the brilliant and demanding Caesar, he was also the only person who could cajole Caesar out of his black moods. He was still very much a hero worshipper, but never a fearful hero worshipper. Caesar often was deliberately inarticulate. He would direct Brooks by pointing a finger, indicating what direction he wanted him to jump.

A friend who ran into them on the street one day recalls Brooks stopping to introduce Caesar to him. Mel talked excitedly about the show, obviously delighted to be able to show off Caesar a little. Sid did not speak. He looked at his watch, then looked at Brooks, and pointed a finger uptown. Brooks suddenly said goodby and walked quickly away behind Caesar.

Brooks and Caesar, both in such a heady atmosphere of success, had come up from the same place. They were two sides of a coin, two heads with the same mind. Today, when he has reason to recognize the enormity of his own talent, Brooks still admires Caesar. "Sid Caesar was a massive talent," he said recently. "He was a messenger full of goodies and little diabolic inside things. I grew up with him. Life was great!"

The competitive system among the writers guaranteed that they delivered their best. But it was impossible in such a situation for a writer to get individual credit for his work. If anyone asked who had written a particular sketch, every writer in the room shouted, "I did."

It was a tough education. Brooks called it Max Liebman University. Its value can be gauged when you consider that virtually each member of the staff made a career for himself after the show died, while other writers of the golden Fifties quickly faded when comedy was no longer king of television. Brooks told journalist Herbert Gold that "those old comedy writers wandered off like atrophied little Jewish spores, waiting . . . waiting for a wetness and a sunniness to make them blossom again." But not Caesar's writers; they were a unique breed.

The style set on *Your Show of Shows* determined Brooks's future growth as a writer and a director. Material for the show was selected on only one basis: Was it funny? In most television comedy writing, public taste is considered before the writers' or performers' sensibilities. Producers might laugh at the jokes but then conclude that the routines are in questionable taste or too sophisticated for most viewers. On *Your Show of Shows*, Brooks told author Larry Wilde, "whatever made us laugh was the only test of what would go into the hopper. I feel that the audience is always ready to absorb anything you have in your mind. They don't reject it based on their own sense of values." This ultimate trust in the audience would insure Brooks's popularity with the public long after most of his critics had bit the dust.

Undoubtedly Caesar was a hard man to please. But once a joke or sketch had passed his jaundiced eye, there was little question of its success with the audience. Caesar made it happen. In his gifted hands, comedy magic was created.

Caesar was lauded for creating comedy based on the world around him. This was the style developed by Brooks back in the Catskills when he would evolve his stories out of the daily events at the hotel. Reviewers called it "honest comedy," clearly recognizable as an extension of something that happened in everyone's life. For example, Caesar tries to direct his boss to his house by telephone: "Well, where are you now? —No, you better get back on the ferry and take the parkway."

Brooks looked at the world around him and fashioned his comedy out of what he saw in people, not what he saw on other television programs. Caesar was a master pantomimist. His big-featured, mobile face could tell a thousand tales with a lift of one eloquent eyebrow. He was a mimic *par excellence*. In a sketch about a fighter pilot, Caesar played both the part of the airplane and the pilot. Characterization was his strongest point. Who was Sid Caesar? What did it matter? He was whomever Brooks's feverish mind could create. There was no Brooks character so bizarre that Caesar couldn't make it blossom into life. Sid was equally convincing as a woman at her morning toilette, a head-lolling infant, a Freudian psychiatrist just off the plane from Vienna, a British general, or a slot machine.

In contrast to this natural style, Brooks developed a second comedic genre. Based on his own experiences as a misfit in school and in the army, he tried setting down an ordinary sort of fellow in an extraordinary situation, or vice versa. Thus, caveman Caesar confronts a Buick in the streets of modern Manhattan. Brooks would develop this style to grandiose heights in later years, but the seeds were planted here on *Your Show of Shows*.

For the next five years, Brooks's entire life was absorbed by Caesar and *Your Show of Shows*. He made only two independent moves. He wrote a sketch for *New Faces of 1952* and had his first serious love affair. Brooks was still relatively immature as far as women were concerned. He was old-fashioned and inextricably tied to his mother. He has said himself that what he looked for in women in those days was someone to replace his mother. In any case, he believed that the thing to do when you were in love was to get married. He married dancer Florence Baum a few months after they met. For her part, the new Mrs. Brooks thought she was getting a successful young man brinking on maturity. Little did she know that Brooks would be forever brinking, and almost always falling back toward childhood. His success at this time was still predicated on his childhood behavior. Growing up was an event to be avoided at all costs. Probably Florence never understood this fundamental aspect of Brooks's nature. It would be several years before he would be ready, at least in part, to be a grown-up. In the meantime, days and nights were spent with Caesar and other writers on top of the show business heap.

It was a fast, exhilarating life, given to endless nights hanging out in small clubs, and days devoted to the sickening pace of a weekly television show.

The only other writing Brooks did at this time was a sketch he contributed to *New Faces of 1952*. It was a clever satire on *Death of a Salesman* as directed by Elia Kazan, in which Willy Loman's son absolutely refuses to pay attention to his father, the crook. The 1952 edition of *New Faces* was a tremendous hit. Brooks's sketch, however, was overshadowed by the performances of such dazzling newcomers as Eartha Kitt and Ronnie Graham.

Melvin was riding high. But he still felt underneath that he was riding under false colors. His success didn't mesh with his Brooklyn ghetto background. "Have they found out yet?" his mother would ask when he'd go home for a visit. Kate couldn't imagine that anyone would pay a twenty-five-year-old man one thousand dollars a week for being as silly as her Melvin. Neither did Mel. One of these days, he thought, they're going to find out that I'm really a jerk, just like everyone else.

# 3

# Crazy at the Top

For five years *Your Show of Shows* led the pack in television ratings. Caesar was supported by a brilliant cast of players including Imogene Coca, Carl Reiner, and Howard Morris. Unbeknownst to Morris, there was a certain amount of friction between himself and Brooks. When Liebman was looking for a supporting comic for Caesar, Brooks wanted the job. Morris, a glib-tongued master of foreign accents and double-talk, was hired instead. While Brooks had nothing against Howie personally, he didn't care much for him on principle. He frequently made Morris the butt of his practical jokes, holding him up in an alley and stealing his wallet. Brooks was so convincing as a holdup man that for months Morris thought the writer actually had momentary lapses of memory where he changed personality. He was convinced that Brooks was a Jekyll and Hyde.

The regular cast of *Your Show of Shows* was aided by a chorus and ballet, as well as by guest stars such as Gertrude Lawrence, Rex Harrison, and Jose Ferrer. A year after the show began, *Your Show of Shows* won four Sylvania Awards

—Best Television Review, Best Director, Best Actor, and Best Actress.

The saga of *Your Show of Shows* hinged on the relationship between Imogene Coca and Caesar. Coca, as she was known to her friends, had been in several Broadway shows in the 1930s and 1940s. She was considered an insider's comic. Each of her performances was greeted with enthusiasm by the critics, but she was believed too "special" for broad audience appeal. Coca was working a standup act in nightclubs when Liebman hired her for the *Admiral Broadway Review*. At one time she had been part of a stage team with her husband, Bob Burton. After the war, however, the Burtons faced a few hard facts. It was clear to Bob that Coca was star material. He decided to quit performing himself and put all his efforts into helping build her career. Liebman suggested pairing Coca with Caesar in one of the Burtons' old routines. It was an instant success.

When the *Admiral Broadway Review* became *Your Show of Shows*, Liebman signed both Coca and Caesar. Rubber-faced, versatile Imogene could switch from a prim Victorian to a stripteaser to a Wagnerian Valkyrie without missing a nuance or a laugh. The wistful little comic was a perfect foil for madman Caesar. Perhaps too perfect to suit Sid. He had always considered himself a single. He didn't mind being supported by another player, but he didn't like the idea of his name linked, back to back, with a partner. As *Your Show of Shows* grew to national acclaim, Caesar and Coca became forever locked together in the public eye. An estimated twenty-five million people tuned in to see them each week. Each comic was given solo sketches on the show. But the routines everyone looked forward to were the duos. So delightful were Caesar and Coca as a team that people across the country thought they were married to each other.

It was shocking then one afternoon in February of 1954 when Caesar called a press conference and announced that he and Coca were splitting up. Years later Coca revealed that she had known nothing about the press conference and had been summoned into the room at the last minute. Asked by reporters why the successful partnership was ending, Caesar said, "It's really a heart-breaking thing. *Your Show of Shows* has been the cradle of great talent. But when a star starts to grow there comes a time when he has to go on his own." Now, he said, it was only fair that each should have his own show. Asked if she agreed, Imogene said, "Oh, I suppose that's quite true." Then she broke down and started to cry. Reporters noted that the only dry eye in the room was Caesar's.

The split wasn't due only to Caesar's ego. For the last year *Your Show of Shows* had been falling behind in the ratings. Network television was not yet aware of the phenomenon of overexposure— that viewers simply got tired of seeing the same people year after year, no matter how good they were. The hour-and-a-half show seemed to burn up material. It was impossible to maintain and surpass the extraordinarily high standards established by the staff. In addition, Caesar felt that much of his material was sacrificed to Liebman's musical production numbers. There had to be time for Imogene to do solo sketches, time for Caesar, and time for Liebman.

Caesar was so eager to get out of *Your Show of*

*Shows* that he took a cut in salary. Sid, at twenty-five thousand dollars a week, had already signed a new ten-year contract. At the time of the split, Coca's contract, at ten thousand dollars a week, was running out. She wondered if the break-up spelled her permanent retirement from television. NBC was willing to take a chance on her popularity without Caesar and signed her for a half-hour show. Liebman also went his own way, continuing to produce *Your Show of Shows* with other stars and developing spectaculars for NBC.

The one-hundred-and-sixtieth performance of *Your Show of Shows* was heralded by a spread in *Life* magazine and in almost every newspaper in the country. Imogene wept throughout rehearsals. Moody and silent, Sid chewed on his cigar. On this last show they repeated one of their most famous skits. A parody of old movies, it cast Carl Reiner as a sweatshop boss, Coca as the consumptive heroine, Sid as her fidgety sweetheart. The overworked heroine faints on the floor of the sweatshop. Reiner, whose intentions are leeringly evil, carries her to his private office. There her poor life slowly ebbs away. In the final scene, Imogene as an angel soars from the set as Sid bows his head in grief and the villainous Reiner crumples on the floor conscience-stricken. The hero sobs as Imogene flies off on block-and-tackle wires wearing big pink wings.

They also repeated several other of their most popular skits. At the final curtain, the cast took its bow. Coca, fearful all day that she would break down, managed to say a few words of thanks to the vast audience. Sid put his arm around her and bit his lip. Whatever his motivation for destroying their partnership—personality clash, oversized

ego, or the economics of network television—
Caesar clearly felt mixed emotions at the ending
of *Your Show of Shows*. At a big cast party after
the show, a depressed Sid joined the band and
played his saxophone.

With Liebman out of the picture, Caesar made
Brooks his head writer and plunged into directing,
producing, and writing his own show. NBC
furnished a lavish suite of new offices at a reputed
cost of one hundred thousand dollars in the pent-
house of the Rockefeller Building. The office had
room for a staff of forty. The show's dancers re-
hearsed on the private terrace surrounding the
office; one floor below was the rehearsal hall
where the permanent cast of twenty practiced
routines.

Ruling over this skyscraper kingdom was the
most successful comic in the world. Caesar com-
manded everyone, from his private butler to musical director Bernie Green. The only person he
seemed to trust was Brooks. The first *Caesar's
Hour* debuted in October of 1954. Caesar, more
brilliant than ever, brought down the house. If
anyone had had any doubts about his ability to
pull it off alone, they kept quiet about it.

Imogene, on the other hand, hated her new
independent state. Given a half hour show of her
own, she told friends, "Maybe I'll get sick or have
an accident." She took little interest in planning
her first show. She was listless, nervous, and unhappy. While Caesar seemed to thrive on the pressure and strain of a weekly solo show, Imogene
suffered agonies of tension. On the day of the
airing she could neither eat nor sleep. Exhausted,
tearful, fighting overwhelming stage fright, she
gave it her best. It was not a success. Her weekly

program format was continually altered in the hopes of finding the right kind of show for her, but after two seasons, she left the air.

Caesar, flying as high as ever, blasted his way into the number one spot in the ratings and held on tight. Trying to keep up with the tail of the comet, Brooks reached a peak of productivity during these years. Even the weekly Caesar show didn't provide enough outlet for his energy. But was all of his thrashing around "creating" sketches really a demonstration of talent? He may have had some idea at this time that if he could write a Broadway show he could really believe he was good. Although he had made a lot of money in television, his name was unknown and unsung in public. Every time he picked up his pay check he still felt he was robbing a Brinks money truck.

Mel got together with writer Joe Darion and collaborated on the book for a new musical based on Don Marquis's popular fantasy *archy and mehitabel.* The sardonic fantasy of two victims of the tides of fate, archy the cockroach and an alleycat named mehitabel, was difficult material to transform into a Broadway play. They were only moderately successful in their goal. *Shinbone Alley,* as the Broadway version was called, received tolerable reviews. Its two stars, Eartha Kitt as the raffish mehitabel and Eddie Bracken as archy, were winning. Together they had one show-stopping song called "Flotsam and Jetsam." But the book received little recognition from critics. It was back to the anonymity of television writing for Brooks.

There is a peculiar dichotomy in writing. The biggest moneymakers are often the least well-known to the public. In the 1950s, film writers and television writers were unknown names. Yet they earned vast sums for their work, far more than most playwrights or novelists could ever hope to see. So while Brooks was frustrated on one hand, on the other he was making so much money that he felt little pain. His value, while unrecognized by the public at large, was appreciated within the select circle of the famous and powerful people of the television industry.

There is no doubt that the chemistry between Caesar and each of his writers was a rare and perfect thing. He turned them on, and they returned the favor. They also did it for each other. It was a multi-cornered affair, built on screaming fits of helpless laughter. Material was used on the show if it passed the Hysteria Test. If everyone at the pitch session rolled on the floor, clutched his sides, wept, howled, vomited, *that* was a joke. If you failed to get a laugh in that kind of situation it was the worst kind of humiliation. The competition was lethal and the judgment merciless. But it drove them all to new heights every day. And in this cageful of lunatics, Brooks was the acknowledged champion madman. More than one of his old friends from those days has paid him the ultimate compliment of saying, "I love him. He's really insane."

They were trying to make the ultimate joke. If any respectable doctor could have laid eyes on that group, he would have ordered them all shot full of therapeutic Benzedrine and tied in straight jackets. They were so naturally speedy that any drug ever invented could only have calmed them down. In any other setting, you would have pitied them. Instead, they were on top of the world. They were great talents, and Caesar was the

greatest talent of them all. Each and every one of
the group idolized Caesar. Says Brooks, in all
seriousness, "Sid had the profile of a silent movie
star."

Then the world trembled. In 1958, the willful
Caesar suddenly walked out on the show. Although acknowledged as the best comedy show on
television, the expensive *Caesar's Hour* was being
beaten in the ratings by, of all things, *The Lawrence Welk Show. Caesar's Hour* cost one hundred and ten thousand dollars a week to produce
in those days, and NBC was having trouble
finding a sponsor to foot the bill. When Caesar
was asked to cut back on production, he refused,
and walked out on the show.

Caesar sat out the summer in silence. He refused to budge on the quality of his program.
While he floundered, the situation sparked reams
of newspaper space and public clamor. Viewers
organized, calling themselves "The Committee for
Caesar's Longevity." One viewer group bought
paid newspaper advertisements in which they
asked: "Do we get Caesar or throw away our TV
sets?"

It was clear that Caesar was trying a last-ditch
effort to keep the show on the air. Although
*Caesar's Hour* had begun as a solo venture for
Sid, it soon was apparent that he fared better with
a supporting cast. He had been through format
changes and new supporting players. Caesar had
been "married" to Nanette Fabray and Janet
Blair in an effort to find an adequate substitute
for Coca. Both Fabray and Blair were well received on the show, but neither was intended as
an equal partner for Caesar. He did not wish to
repeat his role of co-star. But as he sat out the

summer in self-imposed silence, it became clear that he needed a new wedge to reestablish himself at the head of the line at the network.

Aware of the constant public demand for a renewed Coca-Caesar partnership, Brooks designed a new half-hour show. Sid telephoned Imogene and in a tear-choked chat won her consent to their television reunion. Then he called NBC and offered a "reasonably" priced half-hour series with the old Caesar-Coca team. The new program aroused so much interest in the industry that immediately all three networks began bidding for it. ABC won out. "Now I can relax," announced Caesar. "Television is where I belong. It's where I like to experiment. When ABC executives showed enthusiasm in the things I want and hope to do in television we had a deal." Imogene's only comment: "He does all the talking for us."

The new show, called *Sid Caesar Invites You,* was eagerly anticipated by viewers all over the country. Expectations were so high that the opening-night show could not begin to live up to its promise. But it was still better than anything else on television. The new show coasted for the next few months on its past glory. But the television business was changing, and the show was dying. Melvin was dying with it.

Through the manic ups and downs of the Caesar years, Brooks lived through an insanity of his own. Accustomed to winning approval for uncontrollable behavior, even he was overwhelmed to realize that he was getting paid for it, and getting paid royally. The more manic he was, the higher his salary. But he wasn't hanging around on street corners anymore. He was in an enclosed office, premeditating the biggest hit on television, hatching the golden egg that fed all the big guns at the network, creating a show that was seen by twenty-five million viewers all over the country. He had gone from a small-time Brooklyn kid whom no one had ever heard of to the highest-paid writer in the television industry.

When the Caesar mountain began to collapse, Mel, who still felt he was in the world under false pretenses, grew shaky. Writer, they called him. The word terrified him. In literary terms, comedy writing isn't writing at all. As a writer for the Caesar show he jumped up and down, screamed, said anything that came into his head. That wasn't writing. Was it? The more he did it, the more they paid him. But when he had tried legitimate stage writing he had failed.

He had just turned thirty and was rich beyond his wildest dreams. But he didn't know who he was or where he was. He was crazy Mel Brooks. Mel who? The pressure was so intense that his energy level would rise, boil up, and spill over. Mel would dash out of his office and into the streets of New York, running. Running the way he had in the narrow streets of Williamsburg.

Comedy writing is built out of raw, frayed nerves and swollen egos. As Brooks rolled into his ninth year with Caesar, he took to vomiting. Well, everyone on the show threw up. Even Caesar threw up regularly.

The show was fabulous. Yes, truly fabulous in everyone's definition. It was creative, artistic, superlative—and, God help them, the public adored it. The Caesar show's legend was so powerful that even today, twenty-five years later, *Your Show of Shows* and *Caesar's Hour* are remembered with admiration all over the world.

But if it was so wonderful, why was Melb'n such a mess? Why couldn't he keep a tuna fish sandwich down? Why was his marriage on the rocks? Why couldn't he carry on a simple conversation with an ordinary person without stamping his feet or jumping on the furniture? Why was his sleep, on the few nights he could sleep at all, rocked by nightmares?

Well, everyone else on the staff was doing it, he would do it too. Off to the psychiatrist. Sessions with his analyst proved as intense and grueling as sessions in Caesar's office. Brooks sweated out his life on the couch, looking for Melvin, looking for Kaminsky, looking for Brooks, and wondering how they all could fit together.

Mel was knee-deep in analysis when the bottom fell out and *Sid Caesar Invites You* was cancelled. Nobody on Caesar's staff—least of all Mel Brooks—thought it was really going to end. He crashed from five thousand dollars per week to unemployed and unemployable. What kind of market is there for a guy whose major skill is being "really insane"? He says that for eighteen months after the show went off the air, he would wake up at six-thirty every morning and bang his head against the bathroom wall. Comedy shows were finished, his marriage was finished, maybe he was finished. For the next four years, "the kid" averaged eighty-five dollars a week. Having spent fortunes in adjusting to success, he was obliged to adjust again to poverty.

Thus ensued the lowest period in the life of Mel Brooks. He was always out of control. It's one thing to be crazy when you're successful. Out of a job, Brooks's manic behavior won him few friends. "It may be funny to see a guy tap dancing on a table top," recalls a friend who knew him then, "but when it's your table that's collapsing under the weight, you're not very amused."

Others remember that Mel could empty a room just by walking into it. "He couldn't stop talking. If there were other performers present, Mel would just take over. Pretty soon people would start to get up and leave."

Certainly Brooks was still associated with the higher echelon of show business. Everyone in the business knew who he was. He still saw the same people he had worked with on the Caesar show. But everyone was out of a job. Survival was once again the name of the game.

During his marriage to Florence Baum, Brooks had fathered three children. Now he was supporting his ex-wife and children, but he had no home to go to. He was living in a fifth-floor walk-up, picking at the dregs of his success. Fresh out of a six-year marriage, he chased any girl in his path.

Even today Brooks claims that sexually he is fourteen years old. Women who knew him then consider fourteen an overestimate. "I'd say about eleven; twelve tops," comments one lady who should know. "Anything that moved, he'd grab it."

Harder for women to bear than his sexual immaturity was his constant need to be the center of attention. "There was never a moment's peace with Mel around. You could be having dinner with him at some nice quiet spot and he'd do bits all evening. One night he jumped up and grabbed another customer to use as a prop. When he was finished with the story, he returned the guy to his table without any explanation. After awhile it wasn't fun anymore, just embarrassing."

Mel Brooks, born loser. But not quite. The same instinct that forced his rise to the surface before was already at work again. This time it would provide a different sort of outlet for his talent. Many evenings Mel and his old friend Carl Reiner sat around and talked. They noodled around doing bits with each other. They worked out party skits which they would perform before any audience they could nail down.

Anytime more than two show business people get together it's an excuse to try out new material. One night Mel and Carl did one of their skits at a party at Reiner's house. Brooks claimed that he was two thousand years old. "Did you know Jesus?" Reiner asked him. "I knew him well. Thin. Thin. Had a beard. Came into the store and we gave him water." Steve Allen was there that night, and pretty soon he was rolling on the floor. Allen convinced Brooks and Reiner to make a record of the sketches.

They didn't have to be asked twice. They recorded the sketches for Capitol, calling their record *The 2000-Year-Old Man*. The *Man* was the defiant invention of a man who loathes the idea of death. Brooks hates death with a passion. His two thousand-year-old "Brooksman" was a distillation of first generation American Jewish domestic wit and wisdom. Awash with Borscht Belt humor, the *Man* is a geriatric loser with a Yiddish accent who invented the wheel but made it square; someone else cropped off the corners and made a fortune. With the *Man*, Mel introduced an expression into the language—the first of many popular "Brooks-isms." Jewish Americans had a word for something or someone who was utterly lovable: he was a "pussycat." Asked if he knew Shakespeare, the *Man* replies: "What a pussycat he was; what a cute beard." Typically the ancient one invested in *Coriolanus* instead of *King Lear*. "Who wants to see all those daughters yelling," he theorized. "It's just like home."

*The 2000-Year-Old Man* was notable for more than its humor. It firmly established Brooks as a performer, and gave expression to what is probably the greatest ad-lib comedic talent in the business. The sketches also fully developed Brooks's major theory of comedy, exploiting the craziness of the moment out of context with the hour. The 2000-year-old man is everyone's favorite uncle or your own grandfather. But he is two thousand years old. Rhapsodizing on his several hundred wives, he is thrown down through twenty centuries of Memory Lane. "One I remember well, the third one, Shirley. A redhead."

Cast in the role of interrogator, a carry-over from the Caesar show, Carl Reiner led Brooks carefully by the nose, from one bit of lunacy to another, trying to trap him into saying something ordinary. Delightfully deadpanned, Reiner helped Brooks glamorize the modern nectarine.

REINER: Most people are interested in living a long and fruitful life, as you have. . . .
BROOKS: Fruit is good, too. Fruit kept me going for one hundred forty years once when I was on a very strict diet. Mainly nectarines. I love that fruit. It's halfa peach, halfa plum. It's a hulluva fruit; it's not too cold, not too hot. Just nice. Even a rotten nectarine is good. That's

how much I love 'em. I'd rather eat a rotten nectarine than a fine plum, what do you think of that.

The two comics celebrated the lament of neglected parents, from the year 1 through 2000.

REINER: I'm afraid to ask the next question. How many children do you have?
BROOKS: I have over two thousand children—and not one comes to visit me. How they forget a father. Good luck to them, let 'em go. Let 'em be happy. As long as they're happy, I don't care. But they could send a note, write, "Howya, Pop?"

These kinds of bits came naturally to Mel. He'd been doing them since he was a kid. For the first time he tried his wings as a performer. There was no Sid to obscure his talent, just himself and Reiner doing their stuff. Their record was released in January of 1961. Brooks's luck was beginning to turn.

The success of *The 2000-Year-Old Man* set Brooks off on a whole new career. He appeared with Reiner on the Ed Sullivan show and dozens of panel shows. "I had to give it up," he said. "I couldn't have my sandwich in peace at Chock Full o' Nuts. People kept coming up and asking, 'Aren't you Mel Brooks?' " Melvin was making a comeback.

Brooks was still haunted by the fear that he couldn't write. He wanted to give Broadway another try. This time he tackled a musical version of Robert Lewis Taylor's novel *Professor Fodorski*. The plot concerned a European college professor who comes to America to teach engineering to a bunch of knotheads and winds up coaching the football squad. The play was called *All American* and it starred the incomparable Ray Bolger.

*All American* was directed by Joshua Logan with music and lyrics by Charles Strouse and Lee Adams. This time Mel was involved in a hit, almost. Bolger's reviews were splendid. Some critics loved the libretto, others were lukewarm.

Mel was at home with satirical wit. His book had solid humor as well as charm, although his name was mentioned in the reviews only when the reviewers chose to single out what they didn't like about the show. Some thought it heavy-handed and pointless. All in all, *All American* was more successful for its cast than for its writer.

But Mel's life was beginning to fall into place. He was learning to roll with the punches. Writing, he discovered, was not a steady climb from bad to good. A writer doesn't start out at the bottom and by application work his way to the top. He succeeds and fails, and succeeds and fails again. Brooks wrote the highly rated *Caesar's Hour* at the same time he wrote the flop *Shinbone Alley*. And *The 2000-Year-Old Man* was done in the same period as *All American*. Life was up and down. He was learning that he, personally—Mel Brooks—didn't have to cry his own heart out every time he failed in public. He learned that he had a right to fail and still retain his creativity. It became clear that success or failure could not be gauged by public or critical standards. What was important was what he thought of himself and his work. He learned these lessons in blood.

Mel credits the most important event of his life to Charles Strouse. Right after *The 2000-Year-*

*Old Man* had been recorded, while Brooks still didn't know where his next paycheck was coming from, Strouse took him along to a rehearsal of the *Perry Como Show* at the Ziegfeld Theater. Brooks remembers the date: February 5, 1961. On stage rehearsing for the show was Broadway star Anne Bancroft. At that time she was the hottest property in the theater, having won two Tonys in a row for *Two for the Seesaw* and *The Miracle Worker*. Mel claims he rushed onto the stage and said, "Hi, I'm Mel Brooks. I could *kill* for you!" After the rehearsal Brooks asked Anne if she wanted to share a taxi, a time-honored New York tradition. From that moment on, he called her incessantly. "He started following me around after that," Bancroft says. "Not letting me out of his sight. Then I did the same and didn't let him out of *my* sight." It was by all accounts love at first glance.

# 4

## Bancroft

Friends call them The Beauty and The Beast.
Anne Bancroft is generally acknowledged as one
of the most glamorous women in the world.
Critics given to restraint have called her the
greatest American actress of the century. As she
reached the heights of theater and film art, her
beauty has escalated to classic proportions. What,
the public wanted to know, is the lady with the
velvet eyes and worldly-wise voice doing with
madman Mel Brooks? Well you might ask. The
truth is that Anne Bancroft and Mel Brooks are
two of a kind.

Bancroft had suffered many bitter disappoint-
ments before she rose to acclaim in the role of
Gittel Mosca in *Two for the Seesaw*. She had
been humiliated by the Hollywood studios and,
like Brooks, survived a desperate period of soul-
searching in her early twenties.

Behind the elegant, world-famous actress hides
a big-eyed Italian girl from The Bronx. Annie was
the middle child of a large family named Italiano.
She was called Anna Maria Louise. Her father
was a patternmaker in the garment district and
her mother worked as a telephone operator at

Macy's. "We were a typical Italian family," she says. "Very lower middle class. Mamma was the boss." There were three Italiano sisters—Joanne, Anna Maria, and Phyllis—and numerous aunts, uncles, and cousins. One industrious family member tallied the relations one day and came up with the impressive sum of eighty-one.

From her earliest childhood, Annie was an introvert as well as a natural showoff, a paradox that exists in her nature even today. Shyness and exhibitionism were alternate currents in her personality. She loved to perform and would do so at the slightest invitation. When she was three years old she sang for the W.P.A. workers on neighborhood street corners. When her vast family gathered on summer weekends for picnics, Annie was always on top of the picnic table with the potato salad. "Singing," one aunt recalls. "What else?"

From her very first Betty Grable movie, Annie wanted to be a movie star. Not an actress—she didn't know what an actress was—but a famous movie star! But the little performer hated school because she was frightened of the teachers. "I hated the oblivion of my identity," she recalls. "I was just one of the bunch." In fact, Annie was often whisked from classroom to classroom and asked to go into her song and dance act. Teachers found her bright, quick-witted, and a bit of a midget egomaniac. Her shyness was hidden by the razzle-dazzle of her performance.

Much of Anne's singing and entertaining was done to please her mother. Millie Italiano was her daughter's biggest fan. Perhaps, Anne believes now, her mother used Annie as a release for her own expression.

When Anne reached high school, she blossomed anew. It was the first of many metamorphoses she would experience in her life. She was a skinny, unruly girl. To supplement her school dramatics class, her mother sent her to modeling school. Overnight, Annie began to pay painstaking attention to her clothes and hair. She introduced glamor to the high school. She became a slick, style-conscious teenager who was more interested in boys than in theater. She says now, "I was very phony in high school. I was terribly shy and I got aggressive to cover up that awful shyness."

Mrs. Italiano was the dominant force in Anne's life. Millie made the decisions and Anne saw no reason to question her. It was Millie more than Anne who wanted a theatrical career for her daughter. Although Annie had vague ambitions to go on the stage, her dreams were given shape by the strength and support of her mother.

When Anne graduated from high school, her parents somehow managed to send her to the Academy of Dramatic Arts in Manhattan. Even at the young age of sixteen, Anne's vitality and forcefulness were apparent. In her final year at the Academy, Anne was discovered by Frances Fuller, one of the teachers and the wife of television producer Worthington Miner. Mrs. Miner brought Anne to her husband. Miner offered Annie a role on *Studio One*. Over the next year, under the name of Anne Marno, she appeared in dozens of live dramatic shows. When another actor asked her to help him out in a screen test, Anne was spotted by Darryl F. Zanuck. The other actor was never heard of again. Some say that Annie, who was much more experienced than her friend, deliberately upstaged him.

Zanuck gave Anne the opportunity to change her name again. From a long list, she chose Bancroft because all the other names sounded like Lana Turner—"you know, Lana Lamarr, Hedy Hayworth."

Anne was nineteen years old when Zanuck discovered her. While she was being given the starlet buildup at Twentieth Century-Fox in Hollywood, she dated an endless string of eligible bachelors. It was the first time she had lived away from the rigid supervision of her mother, and she enjoyed every minute of her new freedom. "I wasn't unhappy in Hollywood at the beginning," she recalls. "It was a nice life. I'd never had a swimming pool at my front door. I'd never seen a palm tree, and it had never been spring all year round."

At this early stage of her career, Anne was a purely instinctual actress. "I learned my lines. Then they said move here and move there, and I did. And they said bark, and I barked, or, you know, whatever they'd tell me, I'd do." She would not discover the creative force of her work until many years later. But she did absorb her mother's drive and ambition. The ambition seemed to be related to achieving success, but it had a random quality to it. Fame without focus.

Surrounded by Hollywoodiana, Anne's ambition grew to fanatical proportions. She suffered from an aggressive, driving personality in conflict with a quiet inner soul. She wanted to be famous, but she also wanted to have a home like her mother and sisters. Soon bored with dating, she decided she wanted to get married. "Just about anybody would have done," she says.

When a young Texan named Martin May proposed, Anne married him. May was a part-time law student with an oil-rich mother. Thus outfitted with a movie star contract and a rich, good-looking husband, Anne was satisfied that all her girlhood dreams had come true.

Over the next few years, however, the fantasies of her youth didn't mesh with the reality she found herself living. May, she learned, always slept with a gun under his pillow. He was dominated by his mother, even more than Annie was influenced by her own mother. Further, May had little ambition of his own and found Annie's drive impossible to understand. Anne didn't understand it herself. Ambition was consuming her, but ambition for what?

Her six years in Hollywood were a disaster, both professionally and personally. She was too young to handle everything that was happening in her life. Her personality, always complex, had disintegrated. The two distinct sides of her nature baffled her husband. May said of her then, "She was either a hungry tiger or a lovable lap dog."

As an actress, Anne had extraordinary intensity and power, even in the mediocre parts she was assigned. Actors she worked with recognized her unusual potential, but producers were looking for only one type of actress at that time—photogenic blondes with sexy bodies. Anne admits that at first she would do anything to achieve stardom in Hollywood. If cheesecake was what they wanted, that's what she gave them.

Anne made a string of Grade B movies, beginning with *Don't Bother to Knock,* famous now only for introducing a sensitive Marilyn Monroe. This flop was followed by several melodramas and endless Westerns. For one movie, *The Last Frontier*, Anne even became a blonde.

The initial thrill of being a movie star lasted through the first dozen films. After that, Anne began to find her work empty and unrewarding. She would no longer cooperate with the studio, refusing to pose in bathing suits. "I loved the weather in Hollywood," she says, "but I was so mixed up there that I didn't notice the weather after awhile."

Her marriage to May ended in divorce. Free once again, Anne no longer enjoyed the life of a Hollywood bachelor girl. "One can always be popular with boys," she says, "but the rules are different in Hollywood than in The Bronx. Out there you play for keeps."

Hollywood was not the place for Bancroft. She was learning something about her ambition. Success wasn't what she wanted after all. She recognized for the first time that her powerful drive could only be satisfied by the work itself rather than public acclaim.

After seventeen movies it became clear to her studio bosses that Anne wasn't star material. She had two choices: She could continue in Hollywood and have a diminishing career playing Indian maidens, or she could go home.

Anne slid into the low point of her life. She had, in her own words, gone "steadily downhill in terms of self-respect and dignity. I was so unhappy and so lost."

Annie returned home. She moved back with her family, floundered, studied at the Actor's Studio, saw her analyst, and prayed to get the role in the Broadway play *Two for the Seesaw*.

Anne's portrayal of Gittel Mosca, the Greenwich Village beatnik who falls in love with a lawyer from Nebraska, was a milestone in theater history. Few actresses have ever made such an impact in a single role that their careers were safely established for the rest of their lives. *Seesaw* made Bancroft a star overnight.

The characterization of Gittel triggered a vogue for the word "hoyden"; that disarming image clung to Anne for years. As a result, she gained a reputation as a prankster and a "kook." It was generally known that she auditioned for the part wearing a baggy sweater and skirt and black leotards; the first words out of her mouth were, "Ya' gotta john here?"

Anne continued dressing like Gittel offstage during the run of the play. Many people believed that her own personality was identical to Gittel's. Known for her refreshingly direct manner, Anne lent substance to the rumors that she was a nut by giving fraudulent press interviews. But she was even honest about that. "I just tell lies," she said, "and it livens things up a little." When one reporter said that he had heard she was careless with money, Anne said she certainly was not, and took a bite out of a twenty-dollar bill.

Although her offstage persona was a put-up job to some extent, Anne clearly was attached to Gittel. She still feels that any strong role changes the actor who plays it—that the actor is somehow affected for the rest of his life. Anne may have put herself into Gittel, but more than that, Gittel became a part of Anne.

Gittel Mosca was the best-loved character in New York that year. And Anne Bancroft was the best-loved actress. Her notices were universal raves. The ex-Hollywood starlet was awarded the 1958 Tony for her performance.

Many people thought that Anne was too unpolished to play any other role than Gittel. While she received tremendous recognition for her ability, there was still the possibility that Bancroft could be a one-shot actress. Anne dispelled all doubt. She followed up her first stunning success with a second, even more powerful, vehicle—William Gibson's *The Miracle Worker*. With these two plays, Anne Bancroft became the foremost actress of the American theater. She was ranked with Geraldine Page, Kim Stanley, and Julie Harris. Anne captured her second Tony in a row in 1960.

Anne Bancroft was the most famous, most exciting, most sought-after woman in New York City and half the world. Crowds of admirers clung to her in the street. Praise, both critical and public, was heaped upon her from all corners of the world. She was a star of the highest order. It was at this time of glorious achievement in her life that she ran into down-on-his luck Melvin.

The merger is not as odd as it seems. Professional glory aside, Anne freely admitted that she was a flop as far as men were concerned. She had a string of admirers that included Scott Brady and Mario Ferrari-Ferreira. At the peak of her greatest success she told *Time* magazine, "I don't know why, but I can't make a mature relationship based on trust, respect, and recognition." She blamed herself for her romantic failures. "I inevitably invest in people qualities they don't have. And so many times I wind up disappointed." Anne very much wanted to get married again, but something always got in her way. When she told her psychiatrist that she had put a piece of a friend's wedding cake under her pillow, he answered ironically: "At last you're taking active steps."

Behind her fame, Bancroft lived modestly in a Greenwich Village brownstone. She was seldom mentioned in gossip columns and rarely went to parties. "If I open a bottle of champagne with one other person," she said, "that's a party." She had a few close friends, but wished no acquaintances. She saw no purpose in superficial relationships. Her close friends included Arthur Penn, director of *Seesaw* and *Miracle Worker*, Fred Coe, William Gibson, and Jerry Orbach.

Anne's trouble with men, besides her own reluctance to get involved, stemmed from the intensity of her personality. Although many men were attracted to her, few were able to grapple with her strong, demanding nature. And Anne did nothing to cover it up. There were no games to play with Anne, no rules to obscure real feelings. She has been called as transparent as a pane of glass. Her personal vitality was described by one critic as the kind that can turn "red-hot gas grates chilly by comparison." In an attempt to describe Anne's effect on men, her business manager, David Cogan, said: "Men have been hooked by Annie. I don't necessarily mean infatuation. I mean they have been hypnotized. When you are with her, talking with her, she isn't off somewhere in the clouds. She's right there, and she's entirely yours."

This availability coupled with her startling intensity was difficult for many people to accept. When Bancroft met Brooks, she was looking and he was lost. Mel was a man who could understand and appreciate Anne's ambition. He not only understood it, he respected it. He wasn't in the least intimidated by her fame, talent, or power. Anne's drive, like his own, was hinged to personal fulfillment; there was a corresponding match between her artistic growth and her personal development, just as there was in Brooks. The qualities of openness and strength that made other men tremble, thrilled Mel Brooks.

Brooks and Bancroft were very similar people when they met—sensitive, pseudo-tough, physical, emotional, quick-witted, intelligent, and funny. They were people who experienced life rather than merely contemplated it. They were willing to risk everything—total personal exposure—for the sake of their work.

Anne and Mel both had experienced success, money, unhappy marriages, strong family ties, and hair-brained lifestyles which were inconsistent with their inner feelings. They were motivated by the powerful need to be *somebody*. By the time they ran into each other, the worst was already over. Each was looking for something more than success in the eyes of the world.

Anne admired Brooks for his unconventional view of life. "Mel's so wonderful," she said. "Most people if you pinch them they come out with a conventional 'ouch.' But he never says anything ordinary, he's so alive to the fun of life." She also respected his talent. Before they met, she used to always stay home on Saturday nights to watch the Caesar show.

Brooks and Bancroft went out together steadily for the next three years. They didn't deny their relationship, but in the glow of all the Bancroft publicity they managed to keep their private lives off the front page. They dined quietly in out-of-the-way restaurants in Chinatown and Little Italy, went to the movies, and spent many evenings just sitting around Anne's apartment. Each approached the relationship with caution. "It's true we've been going together for some two years," Bancroft told inquisitive reporters in 1963. "He's my favorite fellow. But we've both had bad marriages—and we're both careful as a result. He's a darling—we have fun together and understand each other, I guess. But when we'll get married—or will we get married—honestly, at this point, neither of us knows."

A few weeks later, however, Anne was clearly more willing to commit herself. Before departing for Spain to accompany *The Miracle Worker* to the San Sebastian Film Festival, she commented, "When you're in love, it's no fun going away. I should be looking forward to this trip more than I am."

The night Anne won an Academy Award for her film performance in *The Miracle Worker*, she was working in a play in New York. With her inspired performance in Brecht's *Mother Courage and Her Children*, Anne established herself as the most powerful actress working in the theater. Critics who had searched for adequate praise to describe her performances in her first two plays, in unprecedented enthusiasm now ranked her with Helen Hayes, Katharine Cornell, Judith Anderson, and Ethel Barrymore.

Anne missed her own Oscar Awards ceremony in 1963. A year later, however, she accompanied Brooks to Hollywood where he received an Oscar for his cartoon short *The Critic*. A spoof of art films, *The Critic* was the brainchild of director-animator Ernest Pintoff with whom Brooks shared the award. Brooks wrote the script and narrated the film in the flat accents of a viewer of modern art who knows enough about the subject to know what is dirty. The film was selected for the Cannes Film Festival. Critic John Gruen heralded *The Critic* as "a new kind of movie cartoon—sophisticated, funny, and informed with a civilized malice." Melvin was coming into his own.

Throughout the Hollywood trip, Brooks and Bancroft were questioned about their marriage plans. Anne answered in her characteristically direct manner. She was thinking about it, but she wasn't in any hurry. She told Louella Parsons, "I'm at that time in my life, too, where you stop looking for the man on the white horse and settle for another human being."

Bad marriages aside, the possible merger presented other problems. Religion was one. While not a "practicing" Catholic, Bancroft was the product of a strict Italian Catholic upbringing. At the time of her divorce she had tried to have her first marriage annulled on the grounds that May didn't want children, but her request was denied. This left her in the situation that if she married again she would automatically be excommunicated from the church. "There's no doubt that the kind of upbringing I had you don't get over easily," she said. "All my family is very religious. My grandmother is especially concerned about me, because to her I'm not Anne Bancroft, after all, I'm her granddaughter. She feels that an unmarried woman at that age isn't safe. So I have my grandmother's permission to marry again if I want to. That means a lot."

At first Mel also had some trouble with his family. He introduced Italian-Catholic Anne to his mother. "It's wonderful to meet you," Kate said. "Sit down, have some fruit. I've got to go to the kitchen. You'll know me—I'll be the one with my head in the oven."

But there is a natural affinity between Italians and Jews. They are both family-loving people who laugh easily and cry at the drop of a hat. Supercilious anti-Semitic remarks are often unknowingly directed at groups of Italians. And intermarriage between these clannish people is so prevalent as to have been noted as a cultural phenomenon by *The New York Times.* On *The David Susskind Show*, Brooks was asked if he had ever tried to convert Anne to Judaism. "Convert? You gotta be kidding, David, Annie doesn't have to convert—she's a STAR!"

Heading for England to film *The Pumpkin Eater*, Bancroft remained noncommittal on the subject of marriage. "I've got work, I've got love. That's enough, isn't it?" What else would you want out of life?

The Brooks-Bancroft relationship appeared to be on level ground. As Anne had said, work and love were enough for anyone. Brooks, who had three children by his first marriage, was a dedicated family man, but he sorely missed having his children with him. Anne also had a strong desire to have a family. These family leanings pushed them toward marriage. The affair reached a turning point while Anne was filming in England. Weekends found Brooks winging his way—terrified—across the Atlantic to be with her. Every other weekend for three months. Back at Anne's house on Fire Island in the month of August, both families were visiting. Mel and Anne maintained separate rooms. Mrs. Italiano and Mrs. Kaminsky were on the best of terms. Looking for an excuse to force themselves into going through with the marriage, a hesitant Anne and a nervous Mel decided the situation was too embarrassing for their parents. They had to get married for the sake of Kate and Millie.

The decision was an enormous one for both of them. This was no thoughtless youthful marriage. It was a commitment by two adults to dedicate their lives to each other. It was, for clownish Mel and joke-loving Anne, serious. And so they were married on August 5, 1964, at City Hall, New York City.

Mel's career was beginning to bloom. *The 2000-Year-Old Man* album was outrageously successful. All across the country, Mel Brooks and Carl Reiner were household words. Like so many later Brooks creations, a cult was forming around *The 2000-Year-Old Man*. Mel was the proud recipient of an Oscar for *The Critic*. And the biggest success of his career thus far was about to be born.

# 5

# Rebuilding

Brooks was rebuilding his career. His Academy Award for *The Critic* had earned him new respect in the entertainment field. In the early 1960s he wrote television sketches for several variety programs, many of which were singled out for special attention in the press. Meanwhile, the popularity of *The 2000-Year-Old Man* album continued unabated.

From time to time, bits and pieces of the record were aired by William B. Williams on his popular New York radio program. One lucrative side effect was that the executives at Young and Rubicam, the advertising agency for Ballantine beer, heard the recording. They were sure that if they could harness Brooks they could find a use for his talent in commercials.

The agency people convinced Brooks to sit down in front of a microphone and ad lib. They invited Dick Cavett, in the role of interrogator, to join him. Brooks and Cavett were an ideal pair. Mel declared that Cavett was the most "incredibly gentile" person he had ever seen, and thought the juxtaposition of himself with the blond, all-American WASP was very effective. Besides the paradox

of their distinctly opposite personalities, Brooks
saw Cavett as the perfect foil because, according
to Brooks, Cavett was innocent, guileless, and
aching to be cut to pieces. During the recorded
interviews for the series of commercials, Cavett
would get uncontrollable giggling fits when Brooks
called him "company rat," "pusher," "marshmal-
low," "fluffy," and "sellout."

When they worked together, Cavett would begin by throwing seemingly pointless questions at
Brooks. Brooks would take off on one of his zany
ad libs and Dick would start to laugh. As usual,
Brooks was inspired by laughter. Smacking his lips
over the client's beer, Brooks rhapsodized, "My
tongue just threw a party for my mouth!" Cavett
broke up. Madison Avenue went crazy. They
taped the spot with Cavett's laughter intact.

"You can put a thousand copywriters in front
of a thousand typewriters for a thousand years and
never come up with that line!" said one Young
and Rubicam copywriter. "That's why you have
a Mel Brooks. Because he can give you that flash
of genius. He doesn't use punch lines so much as
he uses startling non sequiturs which get better
with repeated hearings. It's much more long-last-
ing than the typical comic type of surprise-ending
humor." The agency said that "a basketful" of
fan mail was coming in daily praising the brew-
master blurbs. "People even want to form fan
clubs."

Overnight, the Ballantine commercials became
advertising classics. They also sold a lot of beer.
Brooks was as pleased as anyone by all this success, and not in the least embarrassed about "going Madison Avenue." He never made statements
about the crassness of commercials; he was glad

to have the money, and obviously considered questions about commercial versus "serious" comedy pompous and silly. Still, there were artistic considerations involved in his decision to do the Ballantine ads. The most important was freedom. Ballantine gave him complete control of the commercials. The script at all times was subject to Brooks's approval—in theory, at least. In truth, they never had a script. At that time, Brooks's performing style was strictly improvisational. Brooks and Cavett started with a premise and then followed wherever it seemed to go. They recorded many hours of tape, but only the few minutes that Brooks approved were ever used on the air.

And now the world was warned. This was Mel Brooks. From the relative obscurity of the writer —putting words in the mouths of others—Brooks himself became famous as a performer. But as a performer, nobody was putting any words in Brooks's mouth. They were all there right at the tip of his tongue, just waiting to be released. He seemed to pour out a stream of unconscious funniness. It was comic genius at work.

As it was, Brooks loved performing. Basically an ad-lib talent, he improvised at the drop of a question. In *The 2000-Year-Old Man* Reiner asked the questions and Brooks had a split-second to respond. Instantly, he had to fully define his ancient Yiddish personality, an entire story line, and a point of view that was unexpectedly funny. The same performance demands were made upon him in the Ballantine commercials. If Brooks hadn't written for Sid Caesar, he almost certainly would have been performing his own material ten years earlier.

Now he was in demand for commercials by every agency in town, and night after night he turned up on television talk shows. Brooks was seldom thought of as a writer, but as a performer, a comic intelligence inventing his material by bouncing it against another comic sensibility, such as Reiner or Cavett.

His talent was improvisational. He never wrote anything down. On the Caesar show he never learned to type because he noticed the guy who typed was chained to a desk. "I wanted to be the one who ran around and acted it out," he said. Mel just opened his mouth and started talking. His observations were always completely unexpected. He was a natural, intuitive comic who seized a situation in his unconscious mind and produced the gag line to end all gag lines. The best was yet to come. Now he began to put together the purely ad lib, helter skelter, accidental nature of his comedy with a well channeled, deliberately invented and executed written style.

The original idea for *Get Smart* came from producers David Susskind and Dan Melnick. Brooks and Buck Henry were brought in to develop the "approach." Given a free hand, the two comedy writers decided to create a new style of satire based on the already-satirical James Bond thrillers, but more naturalistic in tone. *The Man from U.N.C.L.E.* had begun in this vein, but Brooks felt that *U.N.C.L.E.* fell short of satire. The characters were too human to poke fun at.

Ironically, the ABC network advanced the initial seed money for *Get Smart*. When the first script was submitted, network executives said it was "too wild." Bouncing the script back for

revision, program chief Edgar Schrick told the
writers he wanted something more "warm and
human." Said Brooks: "The executives who read
the script wanted to put a print housecoat on the
show. Max [Smart] was to come home to his
mother and explain everything. I hate mothers on
shows. Max has no mother. He never had one."

Schrick responded that if a mother was impossible the show should at least have a dog. The dog
was intended to give the show heart. So Brooks
and Henry rewrote the show and included their
version of a dog—Agent K-13—surely the mangi-
est, dumbest dog that ever chased cars and bit
strangers. Brooks claimed the dog was merely
"asthmatic." The network wasn't amused. The
dog was out and so was the show. Ten days after
ABC abandoned *Get Smart*, NBC picked it up.
From then on, *Get Smart* had neither man's worst
friend nor a mother.

Months before its premier air date, word passed
through the television industry that the best pilot
of the new season was *Get Smart*. In the original
episode, audiences were introduced to Maxwell
Smart, Secret Agent 86. Smart's enemy is something called KAOS, a foreign agency which has
infiltrated the U.S. training school for spies. KAOS
sabotages everything from munitions to meals.
When the desperate call goes out for help, someone advises the beleaguered U.S. agents to "Get
Smart." Max shows up in the role of a recruit.
The other recruits and the commanders don't
know he has been sent to break up the KAOS
saboteurs, which poses a terrible problem: Max
flunks all the tests he must pass before he can
finish his sleuthing. On the one hand, Smart—
supposedly trained by our top-secret agency known

as CONTROL—is adept at judo and karate, and speaks several languages. But he is also the most inept, stupid, bumbling, hopeless secret agent extant. He survives by confounding the enemy with his best weapon—stupidity. He also has the assistance of Secret Agent 99, a velvety tigress played by Barbara Feldon. Smart only accidentally subdues the villain while muttering things like, "If he could only turn his evil genius into—niceness."

Maxwell Smart was played by Don Adams. "Smart has little piggy eyes," wrote a reviewer for *Time* magazine, "a voice that sounds like a jigsaw on slate, and a perpetual self-satisfied smirk. When challenged, he is too dumb to panic, bluffs fluently: 'Would you believe that I can break eight boards with one karate chop? No? Would you believe three boards? Would you believe a loaf of bread?' "

*Get Smart* had many moments of pure inspired fun, such as the bumbling Max shooting his way out of a closet that he had locked himself in. The show thumbed its nose at all the rules of television programming. It was offensive to minorities, awash with sick jokes, and had an idiot for a hero. The show violated every tested standard of TV comedy. The second episode featured a one-armed Chinese (The Claw) with a magnetized prosthesis. When The Claw asked Smart, "Do you know what they call me?" Smart thought it over, replied: "Lefty?"

Critics raved over the first two shows, but reserved opinion whether or not the writers could maintain the novelty for an entire season. They could have saved themselves the worry. *Get Smart* was an unqualified success. By October, the program was number seven in the Nielsen ratings.

Brooks recalls, "I was sick of looking at all those nice sensible situation comedies. They were such a distortion of life. If a maid ever took over my house like Hazel, I'd set her hair on fire. I wanted to do a crazy, unreal comic-strip kind of thing about something besides a family. No one had ever done a show about an idiot before. I decided to be the first." Because the program was committed to being a satire, Brooks felt that the most bizarre events on *Get Smart* would be accepted by the public, unlike situation comedy which was confined to being "real."

"It's a funny bird," he said. "It's the Big City Protest. It's the only witty show on TV today. Other shows on TV haven't a modicum of wit. They may be funny, but they depend mostly on visual gags. 'Lucy,' for example. Just colored cellophane. But we have a great deal of wit, both in the writing and in the direction."

*Get Smart* was, incidentally, a man's show. Most of the TV shows of the time were designed for women, but Brooks and Henry created *Get Smart* especially for men. They didn't reckon with the show's broad appeal for children. Once again Brooks introduced new phrases into the language. Every kid on the block, when reprimanded by his mother or father, responded, "Sorry about that, Chief." They drove their parents crazy. Asked a simple question, such as "How did you do on your math test today?" kids across the country would query: "Would you believe I got an A plus? No? Would you believe a B? How about an E for effort?"

The program frequently was criticized for bad taste. On one episode about diet, a fat man is

literally worth his weight in gold. KAOS kidnaps
him and puts him on a diet. Smart is trying to get
him even fatter. The episode, written by Brooks,
was called "The Survival of the Fattest." The
NBC executives, cautious about potential viewer
antagonism, tried to get Brooks to change the title
to "The Survival of the Stoutest," but Brooks explained the pun to them and they, rather sheep-
ishly, allowed it to remain.

Mel and Buck Henry worked together in much
the same way as Brooks had worked with Carl
Reiner and the Caesar staff writers. The two comedy writers never sat down at their desks and
wrote. They would get together and start bouncing
material around, each man acting out the parts.
"We played it together," Brooks said. "By trial
and error we found what worked best."

Not all the *Get Smart* shows were written by
Brooks and Henry. The show had two teams of
writers plus several free lancers. In one interview
at the time, Brooks said that he felt the main
trouble with TV was that so many people get in
the way of what the writer is trying to say. He
alluded to a line from *The Madwoman of Chaillot*.
"There are maybe 1100 cabbage pimps between
what's in my head and what comes out of Don
Adams' mouth. The secret is just to let the cabbage pimps take their pieces of the pie but keep
them from pushing the show around."

By this time Brooks was painfully aware of the
hardships of being a writer in the television industry. "So much skill and trouble and effort goes
into the packaging and selling and marketing of
TV," he said. "But how much goes into the basic
idea of a program? They're all so busy packaging
that they never look around and ask themselves,

'Where is the little redheaded Jew with the quill who is scratching out the ideas?'" He worried that writers weren't appreciated, nurtured, and sought out. Eventually this concern forced him into directing.

But in 1967, Brooks was well established as a major talent in the television industry. With a success like *Get Smart* to his credit, as well as his past experience with the Caesar show, he could continue working in television for the rest of his life. The network gave him free rein to develop any shows he wanted. He was even asked to star in a series of his own. Brooks turned down all the offers. He felt television was too hit and miss, too harsh and demanding on its creative people. He was beginning to see television as a monster that devoured material as fast as a writer could turn it out. Few programs had lasting value because once aired, they were never seen again. Now a part of the industry establishment, Mel joined producer Sheldon Leonard in creating two graduate fellowships at Syracuse University for the study of "Dynamics and Composition of the Television Audience."

In 1967, Brooks received an Emmy for a variety special he had written for Caesar, Coca, and Howard Morris. But he wanted to get out of television for awhile. Brooks had dabbled in films. *The Critic* had been his first effort. He also had written a trailer for a film called *My Son, the Hero*. The movie was a flop but Mel's trailer was a hit. Brooks began to think about the movies.

# 6

# The Moviemaker

Following the tremendous success of *Get Smart*, interviewers constantly asked Brooks what he intended to do next. Like all show business people, he would never admit to being idle. His stock reply was that he was writing a novel called *Springtime for Hitler*, a backhanded reference to Edward Everett Horton's summer-playhouse hardy perennial *Springtime for Henry*.

Brooks had become interested in Russian novels and novelists while writing for the Caesar show. Turgenev, Dostoievski, and Gogol were his idols. Since he had done just about everything else, he decided that a comic novel about a sweet, misunderstood Viennese boy who, at one time, was a good dancer and grows up to be Adolph Hitler would be his next project. What started as something of a joke, eventually became a reality in the shape of a film treatment.

The concept of Hitler as a song-and-dance man did not originate with Brooks. During the 1950s, Hitler satires were plentiful, but not readily enjoyed by the public. Few people besides the more *outré* comedians could find anything funny in such a grim subject. Comedian Will Jordan developed a Hitler routine which described the show business powers that were in Germany trying to cast a replacement for the Kaiser. They discover and make a star of Hitler. Lenny Bruce used this same idea and recorded it on his record album *The Sick Humor of Lenny Bruce*, calling it *Hitler and the MCA*. Jordan is still somewhat bitter about Lenny Bruce's use of his material and says that at one time, just after Bruce's album came out, he complained about the theft to Mel Brooks, who commiserated with him. "Then Mel used the material in his *Springtime for Hitler* bit," Jordan says. But he holds no animosity toward Brooks, whom he still admires and considers a friend. "They had been doing Hitler jokes for years on the Caesar show," Jordan says. "I doubt that once he started to enlarge on the idea that Mel thought of my routine at all."

Brooks's musicalized version of Hitler's life was only a pivotal point of a much larger concept. His primary story was about a mother-son love relationship—only the mother is Zero Mostel and the son is Gene Wilder.

Brooks still was not accustomed to putting his ideas on paper. For several months, *Springtime for Hitler* remained a potential novel that Brooks talked about at parties. *Springtime for Hitler* was Brooks's first singular writing effort. Writing had always been for him a collaborative effort, usually done off the top of his head. "When you write for millions of people—TV, movies, recordings—always get a partner. If you write for thousands—a play—maybe get a partner. But for a book written for hundreds if you're lucky, work alone." The self-assigned novel presented him with a lonely task. Writing wasn't so much fun.

Accustomed to being paid for his work, Brooks

couldn't commit himself to actually writing the story until he had professional backing. When he determined that he wanted his story to be a movie, he decided to direct it himself to protect himself from artistic interference. "I became a director in self-defense," he says. "I wanted to control my scripts. I didn't want some other guy—the director—saying, 'Naw, the camera won't be on the girl, it'll be on the chair!' "

Brooks spoke to several studio executives about his plans. Many people were interested in the whacky story line, but not interested in Brooks as the director. Then he met producer Sidney Glazier, who had won an academy award for *The Eleanor Roosevelt Story*. When Glazier first heard Brooks's spoken outline, he fell down laughing and agreed to sponsor the film. "Other producers were afraid he would do it off the top of his head, but I live on instinct, and I had listened to his *2000-Year-Old Man* record and I had seen some of his things with Sid Caesar. He was willing to do it at one-third his normal fee, and I like to gamble, so I went ahead. My cigarette intake tripled."

Glazier raised six hundred thousand dollars for the picture with the remaining five hundred thousand dollars coming from Joseph E. Levine, head of Embassy Pictures, for the distribution rights. Levine was enthusiastic. But when it came time for money to change hands, Brooks found himself in an argument over the right of final cut. Few American directors in 1966 had that privilege. Levine said, "That's my only protection if you don't make a good film."

Brooks, nervous but defiant, refused to do the picture without the right of final cut. There is a peculiar way of thinking among business executives who invest large sums of money in motion pictures. Once the director and actors have completed their work, the executive feels that he has better judgment about the merit of the film than the artists who made it in the first place. He further believes that if there is something wrong with it, he, the moneyman, can fix it by utilizing his right to final cut. Brooks had been brutalized by the television industry. He easily could have continued writing for television at a much higher salary. His main reason for going into film direction was to gain artistic control of his work. As far as he was concerned, there was no point in making the movie if someone else had the privilege of alteration.

The one word to describe Brooks in his negotiations with television and motion picture executives is "defiant." From the days in the Red Bank playhouse he had been unusually sensitive to direction. He stood up to Levine and held a hard line—the right of final cut or no picture. Joseph E. Levine is an unusual man himself. He fully appreciated Brooks's down-to-earth manner. Levine conceded the right of final cut to Brooks. Only afterward did Brooks wonder if he had taken on too much. It was, after all, his first picture. He was temporarily seized with panic, but put it out of his mind to settle down and write his screenplay. Brooks wrote the script, now called *The Producers*, in nine months.

He found it difficult to adjust to writing alone. "You're more unsure writing alone because there's no immediate laughter. If you describe something in a room with five other comedy writers and you get an immediate response, a big scream, then you know you're home with the joke. When you're sitting with just a secretary, you can't go by what she laughs at. If you're sitting alone with a yellow pad and pencil, you can only hear yourself break up. But, if near the end of the writing you can still laugh, you leave the joke in."

*The Producers* was the story of Max Bialystock, a sleazy Broadway producer who raises money for plays by making love to rich little old ladies. Bialystock enlists the aid of his neurotic young tax accountant in a scheme to find a sure flop, raise much more money than is needed to produce the show, and then pocket the excess after the show folds. They decide on a musical comedy called *Springtime for Hitler*—subtitled "A Gay Romp with Adolf and Eva at Berchtesgarden"—written by an unrepentant Nazi who believes that the Fuehrer was infinitely superior to Churchill because he had more hair and besides, he was a better painter. ("He could do a room in one afternoon—two coats.")

To further insure disaster, the producers hire Broadway's worst director, a transvestite named Roger DeBris, and cast a mind-blown hippie called "L.S.D." in the role of Hitler. Their efforts, which include attempting to bribe *The New York Times'* drama critic by wrapping his ticket in a hundred-dollar bill, are to no avail. The whole plan backfires when the play becomes a hit, and Bialystock and the accountant end up in jail.

*The Producers* offered Gene Wilder his first starring role—as Leo Bloom, the wide-eyed accountant. Wilder had made a noticeable impression with his portrayal of a young man who was kidnapped—along with his car and his fiancée—in *Bonnie and Clyde*, even though the part was a small one. He had become good friends with Anne Bancroft when he worked with her on stage in *Mother Courage and Her Children*, and was a frequent guest at the Brooks's summer home on Fire Island. From the very beginning of his screen career, Brooks displayed an unerring instinct for talent. He first approached Wilder about starring in *The Producers* years before the film was ever written. "Mel said to me," Wilder recalled, " 'I've got a great idea for a movie, and you're the only one I want for this part.' Three years went by, and I didn't hear from him; not a message, not a phone call. Then I was in *Luv*, and one matinee day I got a knock on my door and he said, 'You didn't think I forgot, did you?'

"I play a neurotic bud that blossoms into a neurotic flower, a shy guy who carries around a piece of blue baby blanket with him for security. Mel said to me, 'You don't have to act at all, because I got all the people who are just right for the parts.' And I said to Annie, 'Does he really think I'm like that?' She said, 'Just go along with him.' "

Brooks's debut as a film director brought him back into the world of mind-bending pressures. Producer Glazier made the decision that a film so closely tied to Broadway should and could be made in New York City. Tension on the East Coast *Producers* set was spring-tight. Though producer and director decided on a closed-set policy, there were occasional visitors who were admitted. Anne Bancroft frequently came to watch Mel in action. Carl Reiner was always welcome. So was Joseph Stein, who wrote *Fiddler on the Roof*, which had starred Zero Mostel. Playwright Arthur Miller turned up one day and it was only then that most members of the company learned that the production assistant, Robert Arthur Miller, was his son.

Brooks was adamant about excluding reporters from the set. But when *Life* magazine requested a story on the production, Brooks was forced to capitulate. He did not do so graciously. "What do you want to know, honey?" Brooks asked Joan Barthel the day she arrived on the set. "Want me to tell you the truth? Want me to give you the real dirt? Want me to tell you what's in my heart?" Brooks wallowed in antagonism that morning, unleashing his incredible reservoir of energy in a string of bitter invectives hurled at his staff. He sarcastically queried a visiting photographer, "What do you think you're doing? Just what do you think you're doing? Taking a picture of a kid on a pony?"

Was this Mel Brooks being defiant? Was it merely a demonstration of his disregard for established protocol? Or was it the latent resentment of a man who can't bear being controlled by anyone, least of all the executive production company? Had there been a phone call from "upstairs" saying he should do the *Life* magazine interview, or else? Nothing else is a satisfactory explanation for this crude approach to Barthel. Brooks, while admittedly temperamental and subject to nervous tension, is known for his willingness to give time —however chaotic—to journalists. But the day of Barthel's visit, he bristled with hostility.

Had he encountered any problems in directing his first movie, she asked? "No problems at all. I know everything and that's my problem."

Producer Glazier was stunned by Brooks's behavior, but his worried look shot at Brooks made no impression. Melvin, the devil, continued. "I don't know how these lying interviews go. I don't know how to do this. Usually, you say, 'I never thought it would be such a wondrous experience, and everything is fine, and everybody has been so kind to me, and I hope humbly that I am going to do a good job for everybody, and the word around is that it's the best comedy being made in America since the Golden Age of Comedy with W.C. Fields.'

"That's the kind of interview I could give you. But I hate to lie and sound jolly, and I wouldn't tell the truth except to the people I have known and loved for years."

Brooks was clearly working himself up into a rage. "Anyway, what good does it do us now, this story? Save this and give it to me when the picture comes out. If the story came out in November it could be valuable to the film."

Brooks's hysteria by this time extended to everyone on his crew. Glazier asked the reporter, "Pray for me." However much Brooks would have liked to be rid of Miss Barthel, he allowed her to remain on the set to observe a scene being shot.

Zero Mostel and Gene Wilder are squeezed together on a not-too-sturdy green loveseat in the apartment of the man they've chosen to direct the bomb they're producing. Playing the director was Christopher Hewett. Hewett comes out from behind his dressing screen and minces toward them wearing a sequined gown with immense black velvet sleeves lined in electric pink, dangling earrings, and a flirtatious gleam in his eyes. Neither Max Bialystock nor Leo Bloom bat an eye. Max is the first to speak. With all the sincerity he can muster, he comes out with a compliment. "That color brings out your eyes. Let's face it, Roger, that dress is *you*."

Wilder and Mostel play the scene to the hilt, but there is no convulsion of laughter at the end. Brooks calls "Cut!" and leaves the set. Meanwhile, Barthel tracks down Zero Mostel in his dressing room, where he lights a cigarette and turns his best interview style on the reporter.

"It's surrealistic. A satire on show business," he tells her. "A marvelous spoof. The character I play bribes a critic as he walks in to the theater. And in a sense, producers do bribe critics by giving them choice seats, a hot lunch. And I know producers who write off plays, who live on flops deliberately, because even with a flop, they always make money. So this movie isn't that far out, after all."

Mostel, who has the reputation for being impossible to direct, spoke highly of Brooks but inferred that he had reservations. "I always liked the script," he said, "and Mel has great craziness, which is the greatest praise I can have for anybody. You know, that flare-up you saw is part of the makeup that makes him good. My nature is not to take anything too heavily; I make a few jokes here and there, and I bear with it, because it's better than working with a sweet ass who has no talent at all. But someday—someday I'll work with somebody who is both talented and sweet, and I'll die in his arms."

Mostel's inference that Brooks was temperamental had foundation. There is room for only one temperamental soul on a Mel Brooks set, and that person is Brooks himself. His actors are permitted total freedom in front of the camera, but Brooks expects them to turn it off when the scene ends. For his part, he fully supports the people who work for him.

In a final attempt to get the story for *Life*, Barthel once more encountered Brooks—after the lunch break. He appeared more irritated than before. "What did you hope for when you came here? What did you want?" The reporter said that she had no preconceived notions, and Brooks replied with: "That's too vague, too general. You must have had some idea. Or are you just a big blob of cotton?"

*Life* reporters were not accustomed to abuse from the people they interviewed. Before Brooks finished his sentence Barthel was already on the way out the door. Brooks angrily followed her with a parting shot: "Do you fool around?"

Although *The Producers* won Brooks the 1968 Oscar for Best Screenplay, he didn't believe it was a success with the critics. "A lot of movie critics don't like movies enough," he said. In New York, the picture received uncommonly excellent reviews. Most critics, however, liked the first half of the film, but felt it flattened out at the end.

"Unfortunately," wrote the reviewer for *Time* magazine, "the film is burdened with the kind of plot that demands resolution and here Brooks the Writer has failed Brooks the Director. *Springtime* is supposed to be like *Valley of the Dolls*—so excessively bad that it's hilarious. Instead it is just excessive. *Producers* ends in a whimper of sentimentality out of keeping with the low jinks that went before."

Renata Adler, after giving the film a brilliant review in *The New York Times*, also withheld praise from the ending. When the stage version of *Springtime for Hitler* was seen in the film, Adler felt the movie made a "terrible and irreversible mistake. It allows the audience on screen to find the play funny. This turned the real audience in the theater off as though a fuse had blown. Hardly anyone laughed again. Partly, it must be admitted, because *Springtime for Hitler* itself gets less funny at this point. . . . On the whole, *The Producers* leaves one alternately picking up one's coat to leave and sitting back to laugh."

This kind of vacillation on the part of reviewers drove Brooks crazy. He couldn't bear the seemingly rave reviews that in fact contained unmerciful barbs. The public also took exception to the critics. In response to Renata Adler's review in *The New York Times*, one reader wrote: "If one reads between the lines of her masterfully ambiguous review, one gathers she didn't much care for the film. She has every right not to. But as a critic, she owes it to her readers to take some recognizable stand. Having seen the film and having laughed uproariously along with some 400 other people, I can state that this brilliant, honestly funny film is destined to be one of the comedy classics. I could be wrong. But no one could ever accuse Miss Adler of being wrong—or right. Too bad she can't climb off her fence and laugh."

This pretty much characterized the state of critical response to Mel Brooks that would continue through the next several years of his career. Reviewers liked parts of his films, but were unwilling to commit themselves totally to his point of view. Only Wanda Hale, reviewer for the *Daily News*, would unreservedly praise Brooks and continue as one of his biggest admirers. "The last sequence is the funniest of all," she wrote of *The Producers*, "and anyone ornery enough to give it away deserves a hit in the head. Anyone, from whose head came this fantasy with profound undertones, can be forgiven for occasional looseness in direction. But even so, Mel Brooks has done remarkably well with his first feature-length film which is sheer magic."

The spectre of bad taste, which would hound Brooks with each successive film, arose in full regalia in the reviews for *The Producers.* "Some will find Hitler poorly chosen as an object of fun and satire," wrote Archer Winsten. "The fun is really there, but not if the name triggers other emotions too strongly."

Brooks did not suffer the criticism lightly. For the next two years, he claimed "bleeding wounds" from the onslaught of criticism. Even the Academy Award and the knowledge that an audience cult was forming around *The Producers* did little to alleviate the pain. Friends and admirers rushed to his defense. Brooks was especially grateful to Peter Sellers, who screened *The Producers* and the next day took full-page ads in *Daily Variety* and *Hollywood Reporter.* Sellers wrote: "Last night I saw the ultimate film . . . *The Producers.* . . . Brilliantly written and directed by Mel Brooks, it is the essence of all great comedy combined in a single motion picture. Without any doubt Mel Brooks displays true genius in weaving together stage-comedy, comedy-tragedy, pity, fear, hysteria, schizophrenia, inspired madness and a largess of lunacy with sheer magic."

Seemingly overwhelmed by the praise, Mel told reporters, "I want you to know that it's only a little picture, crazy, insane, and I don't care if you critics say it's hilariously funny." There was a rumor to the effect that Brooks had written the blurb himself, with Sellers' approval, and inserted it in the papers as a joke.

# 7
# Twelve Chairs

By the time Brooks approached the script for his next film, he had developed a strong writing discipline. His technique was a painstaking process that involved detailed index cards for each scene. Mel allowed a year for the written script and said that even after the screenplay was bound, it would not be ready to go in front of the cameras for another six months. Describing the six-month period he allowed for revision, Brooks said: "We'll attack that script like we were Nazis in September 1939, entering Poland, that's how fiercely we'll attack that script. And it'll have to act like Israel in 1948, brave and courageous, fighting for its life."

Critics, of course, would never believe that Brooks actually wrote his scripts at all. He was and would continue to be eternally accused of making them up as he went along, inserting jokes on whim with no attention to the way they would fit into the picture as a whole. But Brooks squandered love and attention on the merest detail of each of his screenplays. More and more he was becoming dedicated to writing as an ultimate expression of his art. "I want to grow up to be Sean

O'Casey some day," he said. "That's my dream, to be O'Casey. But until that day I'm in there with the rest, swinging away for a living."

Once more he insisted that he would direct his new film only to protect his ideas. "Most directors try to be funny when they do comedy," he told journalist Brad Darrach. "Disaster! The writer has to be funny. Not the director, not the actor. When I did the Sid Caesar show, the designer would sometimes try to do a funny set. All the writers would rush into his office, throw him down on the floor and sit on him. 'Don't help us!' we would yell at him. 'Make the sets real. We'll do the jokes.'"

Given the protection of writing and directing, Brooks still felt the confinements of filmmaking. "What you're after," he said, "is to make a Mount Whitney of a picture. What you settle for is a wonderful snowball." The time in between was "agony—compression, remolding and restructuring—tension, tension, tension."

Brooks was by this time a self-taught intellectual. He wished to combine a tragic sense of life, surrealism, and an added footnote on the brotherhood of man—mainly observed in the lack of it—in his next film, *The Twelve Chairs*.

*The Twelve Chairs* was not unlike Brooks's very early short story about the rich cat and the poor cat. On the surface, it followed the madcap adventures of three crazy people on the run after hidden treasure; at bottom, it was a story of personal greed and governmental stupidity. Brooks adapted his satire from a story by Soviet writers Ilya Ilf and Yevgenyi Petrov that was published in the 1920s. Asked the theme of the film, Brooks explained, ". . . the common goal government.

Everybody's the same: eternal need and eternal greed."

Ilf and Petrov called their story *Diamonds to Sit On*. It was one of two novels (the second was *The Little Golden Calf*) involving an accomplished con artist named Ostap Bender.

With his usual fine eye for actors, Brooks cast the then unknown Frank Langella as Bender, the appealing con man. Ron Moody played an impoverished aristocrat, and Dom DeLuise was a conniving priest.

The story is set in 1927. Ippolit Vorobyaninov (Ron Moody), once a great nobleman, now works as a petty civil servant in a small town. On her deathbed, his mother confesses that during the revolution she sewed the family jewels into the seat of a gold brocade dining room chair, one of a set of twelve. The family estates and properties have long since been confiscated by the government, but Vorobyaninov, muttering under his breath at both his mother and his fate, sets out to trace the chairs.

He acquires a partner, the resourceful Bender, to help him try to outwit rival fortune hunters, one of whom is a village priest who heard his mother's last confession. The priest's pursuit of the chairs is characterized by ecstatic self-degradation, self-deception, and passionate conferences with God. He sees himself as God's junior partner. There is a scramble by all parties to find the chairs, from the Ukraine to Siberia, from the Black Sea to Moscow. A few at a time, the chairs are located and ripped apart, but they yield nothing but stuffing.

Frank Langella and Ron Moody worked well together as a comic team—Langella as the very tall, tenacious Bender, and Moody, barely reaching his partner's shoulder, as the sad-faced aristocrat. Moody's grave and ridiculous portrayal was the film's symbol of human endurance as well as human folly.

Langella, an actor well-known on the stage but making his first movie, praised director Brooks: "He's one of the few men in the world I would trust with my life."

The high point of the film was Brooks's own portrayal of a happy peasant caretaker at a home for the aged. In happier days, he had been the former aristocrat's former serf and staunch friend in adversity. In one scene, the con man asks the caretaker what goes on in the old folks home. "The old ladies," Brooks answers with no show of emotion, "they tippy-toe in. They have a bowl of porridge, and then they. . . ." Brooks then explodes an abrupt Bronx cheer—a euphemism for kicking the bucket.

Brooks also once more demonstrated his song-writing talents. He had written the "Springtime for Hitler" song in *The Producers*, in which a line of myopic Nazi chorines sing *"Here Comes the Master Race!"* For *The Twelve Chairs*, Brooks borrowed a tune from Johannes Brahms and came up with the ultimate comic lament—"Hope for the Best, Expect the Worst." "I always wanted to work with Brahms," he said of his collaborator. "So it was a real thrill when he agreed to write the music. A nice man, too. A short man, in a wig, but nice."

For outdoor locations, Brooks took his cast to Yugoslavia, a country that resembles Russia in terrain and architecture, with the necessary four seasons for background.

"Yugoslavians tell you they are a happy people," Mel said of the journey. "They put their heads on the table and cry when they are telling you they are happy. Belgrade is a beautiful city, but at night I think they light it with a twelve-watt bulb."

The jokes obscured the difficulties of filming on a foreign location. Brooks struggled with union representatives and language problems with his crew. Although his approach to his second film was considerably more relaxed than the first, he was still demanding and hard-driving. But there were no hard-to-explain scenes with reporters. Mel was his usual boisterous self on the set, but handled all press interviews with a new decorum.

Nevertheless, Brooks couldn't resist a series of Yugoslavian jokes when he came home. "Yugoslavia was fine," he said. "But they had one dish —it just stopped and took up residence right beneath your heart. It became your constant companion, your best friend. You'd call it 'Harold.' Each morning you'd say 'Hello, Harold, how ya doin' in there?' " Mel claimed that several times a week he went to Paris to have lunch.

Jokes aside—"I took one look and thought they must be hiding the country; it's out back somewhere"—Yugoslavia provided lovely backgrounds for the picture. It also provided a first-rate director of photography in the person of Djordje Nilolic. Before he worked with Nilolic, Brooks tended to set up his camera and let the actors run around in front of the lens. He was badly abused by the critics for the amateurish camera technique of *The Producers*. Nilolic showed Brooks what a camera was for. *The Twelve Chairs* drew critical praise for its expert cinematography, as well as its sophisticated use of film technique applied to comedy, such as rushing the camera speed to intensify sight gags.

The set decoration, including interiors and facades of buildings, was done in bright colors with clear outlines. Frantic chases occurred on countrysides full of lovely rolling hills and dales. Dom DeLuise broke a chair in a graceful setting of rocks and seashore. The camera placement, inventive and patient, more than did justice to both the comedy and drama. On their way to the last chair, Moody and Langella take a long walk, with Langella out front and Moody trailing, past falling leaves, over rocks, past tall trees black against the setting sun, and over railroad tracks covered with snow. In the last scene there is a brief shot of several women in dark coats and yellow caps shoveling snow from the sidewalk into the street. Brooks allowed a bit of the artist in him, that tender part of his nature which he protects from public view, to show through in *The Twelve Chairs*.

The Yugoslavian locale also permitted Brooks to bring in his second picture at the low budget of $1.4 million, which in itself assured backers that the picture would make a profit.

A lot of the savings were realized through Brooks's do-it-yourself habits. While some filmmakers like to delegate functions to others, Brooks is dedicated to the old-fashioned idea of overseeing every detail—from writing the script to checking the bulbs in the ushers' flashlights. Also, Brooks got only fifty thousand dollars for writing, directing, and co-starring in *The Twelve Chairs*. It took him three years to make the picture. After the tax bite, he was left with about half of the fifty thousand dollars. For the three years of writing and production, he received eight thousand dollars a year.

*The Twelve Chairs* opened in seventy-two theaters in the New York metropolitan area the week of January 16, 1971.

Gary Arnold, writing for the Washington *Post*, complimented Brooks on his newly acquired photographic expertise, describing the landscapes and setting as having "charming, nostalgic storybook qualities." But Arnold assumed that half the time Brooks's success was accidental.

Stephen Gottlieb of the *Village Voice* reserved praise for Brooks's new film technique: "One swallow maketh not summer," he wrote, "and it takes more than a few beautiful camera setups to put a director in the D.W. Griffith–John Ford–Anthony Mann class of outdoor photography."

New York critics generally agreed that the highlight of the film was Brooks himself in the role of the demented caretaker. Mel wasn't displeased, but took the opportunity to criticize the "crickets," as he called them, because as usual they would say something nice about him, then "take it back."

Vincent Canby, the well-known, rather pompous critic for *The New York Times*, established himself as one of the half-baked Brooks fans. Canby, over the next few years, would insist on comparing Brooks with Woody Allen, with Allen faring far better in the Canby ratings. Most of the action of *The Twelve Chairs* was, Canby felt, "almost as joyless as the Soviet Union the film purposefully depicts. This is, I think, because Mr. Brooks's sense of humor is expressed almost entirely in varying degrees of rudeness and cruelty, unrelieved by any comic vision of mankind, of the Soviet Union, or even of his characters." Following several paragraphs of praise for Woody Allen, Canby closed his review noting that, "Brooks wants to be lovable, and to stomp on your foot at the same time. I, for one, object."

Typical of the semi-ecstatic review for *The Twelve Chairs* was one by Pauline Kael of *The New Yorker*. Kael gave the film her qualified endorsement, noting that the post-revolution Russian setting "gives Brooks an opportunity to show his nostalgic affection for the slapstick and mugging and innocent nuttiness of earlier periods . . . but, gifted as he is, he still doesn't go beyond gag comedy."

Brooks fumed at the reviews. He could not understand how someone could like his movie, but not like it. "I would prefer open outrage or clear applause," he said. "They don't like the movie because they have to grapple with it. The picture becomes not a friend but an enemy."

It was clear, however, that Brooks was becoming a director of some import. The review by Stephen Gottlieb in the *Village Voice* represented the seriousness with which some critics were beginning to take Brooks. Gottlieb wrote: "The difference between making toast and writing and directing a motion picture is one of complexity. A critic of toast can say with confidence that if the toast had been removed sooner, it would have been perfect. But a critic who tells a writer-director that he should have had more of this or less of that is no more likely to be right than a batboy handing out batting tips to the ball players. 'Now Mel, if you'd keep your weight on your back foot a little longer. . . .'"

Gottlieb felt that *The Twelve Chairs* got better as it became less funny. It was not that he believed there were fewer comedy bits in the second half of the film, or fewer serious implications in the first half. "But," he wrote, "comedy rises to the surface in a moment. It takes our eyes longer to get accustomed to the relative somberness of drama. Possibly, if there had been fewer gags in the beginning, if the creator had risked puzzling us, yes, even boring us, one spectator might have realized sooner that *The Twelve Chairs* is less funny but grander than *The Producers*. . . ."

Gottlieb also praised Ron Moody's performance because he felt Moody seemed to do little, yet "everything gets done. The patient close-ups of his face surprise him at the grand moral moments of imperial suffocation, grinding loneliness and friendliness. Frank Langella's unashamed clarity gives Moody the right foreground."

A few reviews, such as the one by Wanda Hale in the New York *Daily News*, a committed Brooks supporter, had only praise for *The Twelve Chairs*. "A Mel Brooks picture is cause for rejoicing by the discriminating," she wrote. *"The Twelve Chairs* is a gem, a bright and unique comedy with humor and heart." Gary Arnold also admired *The Twelve Chairs* outright. "This new comedy is much more consistent and fluid than Brooks's first film. . . . You don't gyrate as wildly between inspired and rather mediocre bits, but the 'wild' bits, the *idées fixes*, are still there, performed brilliantly."

But the majority of reviewers reserved total approval. Archer Winsten, columnist for the New York *Post*, felt that it was far-fetched to suggest that *The Twelve Chairs* was a farce that rose to a higher level of philosophical meaning. But he still enjoyed the humor of Brooks's folk tale. He wrote: "Mel Brooks is a mean man with farce. As the picture begins with a disturbing series of Russian-accented speeches in English, one instinctively rejects the hodgepodge produced with Hungarian peasant faces and British actors. But a change soon takes place. Ron Moody is an irresistible actor, and Frank Langella, the newcomer, is a man of great presence, and Dom DeLuise flowers in farce. Mel Brooks, himself, playing Tikon, a groveling former serf-servant, helps in every way to make the transitions work."

Brooks bitterly defended himself against critics who assumed he made movies in a slapdash, uncontrolled manner. "It takes me two years to make a picture; eighteen months of writing and six in production. Most writers do their story in six months. I can't. I write and rewrite for the kind of comedy I do, keep pads and pencils all over the house, jotting down new ideas and dialogue that comes to mind any time of the day or night."

Brooks had earned a certain respect with his first two major films, but he was not by any means identified as a major filmmaker. His comedic style was still measured against other comedians and other writers. No one had yet seen the possibility that Brooks was creating an original form of comedy, uniquely his own. But in his next film, Brooks would fully develop two comedic genres—the whimsical juxtaposition of time, combined with "honest" comedy and the slightly crooked view of the world around him—into screen dynamite.

# 8
## Blazing Mel

Becoming a national figure of heroic proportions was not Melvin's original plan. He was running out of money and needed a job. A Warner Brothers story editor, Judy Feiffer, had come across a script that she thought Brooks might want to direct. On an off-chance that he would be interested in working from someone else's original material, she sent him *Tex-X*, a story about a black sheriff in the Old West. *Tex-X*, retitled *Black Bart*, had been written by Andrew Bergman. Brooks was immediately intrigued by the possibilities of lining up a character who spoke hip, black, urban lingo against a background of antique Western clichés. "The white characters will keep saying, 'I'll be hornswoggled' and 'They went thataway,' and the sheriff will answer 'Right on, man!'"

Brooks thought Bergman's script could be opened up to broad comic possibilities. He called the screenwriter and asked if he would allow him to perform drastic script alterations. Bergman, showing none of a writer's usual territorial defensiveness, was delighted. But, he wanted to know, could he help? Brooks wanted to work on

the *Black Bart* script the same way he had worked
on *Your Show of Shows*. He called a group of
writers together—Norman Steinberg and Alan
Uger, a comedy team, Bergman, and Richard
Pryor, perhaps the most brilliant writer-comedian
in the business. Brooks and the others isolated
themselves in a single room, turned on the tape
recorder, and started throwing lines from the
script. Pryor, who is black, concentrated on the
Jewish jokes, and the Jewish writers focused on
the black jokes. The same level of hysteria as in
the old television days erupted in the room, but
they had no one to please but themselves. There
was no cut-throat competition, just the pure joy
of five people doing what they most loved to do.
For four months they worked together. Their first
script was 412 pages long, enough for an eight-
hour movie. Fortunately they were refinanced by
Warner Brothers, worked another three months,
and reduced their scenario to 275 pages, still
twice the length of a shooting script.

By this time Brooks was completely in love
with the script. He knew, beyond any doubt, that
in this picture he would fully develop his style as
a director, and he would be able to state practically everything he had to say so far. But it was a big
risk. It was his first film collaboration, and his
first big-budget production. It was a "Hollywood"
picture: big cast, big sets, big money. And "Hollywood" does not determine failure or success on
artistic merit. Profit is the criterion. While neither
*The Producers* nor *The Twelve Chairs* was a big
hit, they both made money. They made money
because the production costs had been kept low
enough to virtually guarantee a profit.

As long as a director makes films that make a

little money, he is practically assured of continuing work in Hollywood. The critics can hate him, but the studios will always find him a place. *Black Bart's* budget was so large that the film would have to be a complete public and critical success to break even. If this movie failed, Brooks risked not ever working in motion pictures again.

But it wasn't the first time that Brooks had put it all on the line. Risk-taking was second nature with him. As usual, he jumped in first and thought about the dangers afterward, just as when he insisted on the right to direct and cut *The Producers*.

It took Brooks two years to get the picture ready for screening. Brooks said of his pending brainchild, "We're trying to use every Western cliché in the book in the hope that we'll kill them off in the process." The plot of *Blazing Saddles*, as it was now called, was a pastiche of clichés from every Western movie made since the days of Tom Mix. Cleavon Little played a black sheriff who is hired to defend a small town against a gang of land-grabbers led by a sneaky lawyer named Hedley Lamarr, played by Harvey Korman. Of course, Little is hired by the lawyer who figures the sheriff will be lynched by the townspeople. The lawyer's girlfriend, a Teutonic singing prostitute with a Marlene Dietrich lisp, was played by Madeline Kahn. Backing the sheriff is an alcoholic fast-draw expert (Gene Wilder). Brooks himself played two roles—a silver-tongued, cross-eyed state governor and a Yiddish Indian Chief.

Brooks wrote some new songs for this film. The title song, "Blazing Saddles," allowed Frankie Laine to satirize himself. Madeline Kahn performed "I'm Tired," which laid waste forever Marlene Dietrich's "Falling in Love Again."

As usual, Brooks's cast of players dedicated themselves to their director. Brooks, unlike some directors, admires actors. He believes his script is in a sense rewritten by the players—not because they improvise lines, but because they bring so much of themselves to the roles. He encourages complete freedom in front of the cameras. "Go bananas" is his favorite stage direction.

As Lili Von Shtupp, Madeline Kahn disarms the sheriff by accepting his gift of a single flower with the immortal words, "Oh, one wed wose, how wovely!" Kahn, the most gifted actress-comedienne on the screen today, claimed that she did not actually impersonate Marlene Dietrich. "My interpretation of the character," she said, "had a lot of me and a lot of Mel Brooks in it, though Mel did want certain references to Dietrich's roles. But it's a parody of films, not of her—films in which a certain type of lady reduces men to jelly." Lili is a heaving sea of bosom and thigh; she sulks, lisps, pouts, and sneers her audience into a state of frenzied lust. "Phooey," she yawns, "go away. The lady is tie-urt."

Madeline Kahn has worked almost exclusively for Peter Bogdanovich and Mel Brooks. Bogdanovich cast her in her first film, *What's Up, Doc?* She played an uptight and generally repulsive fiancée to Ryan O'Neal. She was required to submerge her abundant femininity in an utterly sexless role, but even so, critics saw through the shrewish performance to the comic brilliance underneath. Bogdanovich compensated her for this part with the stunning character role of Trixie Delight in *Paper Moon*—a sexy kootch girl who latches on to a con man. When it came to Mel Brooks, Kahn found herself in a totally different environment. "My audition for Mel for *Blazing Saddles* was . . . intense. It lasted two hours. I felt like I was at the Mayo Clinic. For a funny man, he's very serious."

Kahn is a perfectionist who arrives early on the set and does her own makeup. She relaxes and joins the others only after shooting is completed. Brooks is eloquent on the subject of Kahn's talent, and believes that she is headed for superstardom. No one was more delighted than Brooks when a preview audience of *Blazing Saddles* burst into applause following Kahn's Marlene Dietrich imitation.

Comedy directors seem to be following a pattern of creating their own repertory companies. Gene Wilder, now one of Brooks's most trusted and respected performers, gave a classic performance as the alcoholic good-guy gunman whose speed on the draw was so great he appeared never to move.

*Blazing Saddles* is a lesson in comedy acting. Neither Brooks, Kahn, Wilder, nor Little ever reveal by the merest lift of an eyebrow that they know the situation is peculiar. They play as straight, clean, and well-intentioned as if they were making a Shakespearean tragedy. Wilder's blue eyes have never been more sincere, Brooks never more of an unconscious fool, Kahn never more serious than as a lady who believes in her total sexual prowess, but lisps.

Almost exactly two years from the day Brooks first read the script, *Blazing Saddles* unwound in the Warner Brothers screening room. At the first big joke, Brooks anticipated the laughter. A white cowboy addresses a black labor gang: "How 'bout a good ole nigger work song?" With all the precision and swish of a Fred Astaire picture, the gang breaks into, "I get no kick from champagne. . . ."

There wasn't a sound in the screening room. Brooks claims it was the worst moment of his life. The picture continued to spin out its life, and Brooks's along with it. The Warner executives were grim. *Blazing Saddles* bombed hard.

Brooks couldn't believe it. Had he and the other writers and performers been working in such isolated chaos that they had gone in an entirely wrong direction? Were the cast and crew of *Blazing Saddles* the only ones who thought the picture was funny? Was that possible?

The picture was scheduled for a public sneak preview that same night. Brooks wanted to cancel it, but his assistants convinced him to let the movie roll. At eight o'clock that night, Brooks went to the screening room, expecting to witness the funeral of his career. The lights were dimmed, and Brooks and his whole staff sat on their hands, waiting for the moment when the black work gang starts singing Cole Porter.

The audience fell apart, and continued laughing for the next two hours. Brooks was reprieved. He had been right to follow his own comic instinct and trust the audience. The film was screened again the following night in a different location. The response was overwhelming. People laughed until they couldn't breathe. *Blazing Saddles* was a hit. It was refreshing, original, insane. People loved it.

Why the Warner Brothers' brass didn't like it is still a mystery. Their reaction probably stemmed from the typical method of judging films. Was there anything offensive to minorities? Definitely.

Was it in bad taste? Certainly. Did it make sense? Absolutely not. Did it have a satisfactory ending? It didn't have an ending at all.

Not even Brooks expected the film to have the mass appeal and staying power that *Blazing Saddles* showed. He assumed that the film would have a cult appeal like his other work. He also thought they'd hate it in Peoria—that *Blazing Saddles* was strictly a big-city picture. Yet people flocked to see *Blazing Saddles*. Middle America had already discovered lox and bagels, chocolate sodas, and chopped chicken liver. Brooks's hypothetical Midwestern Protestant, who "drives a white Ford station wagon, eats white bread, vanilla milkshakes, and mayonnaise," had acquired a little bit of funk. "Jewish" humor had finally become American humor. Everybody had picked up on Brooks's *meshugaas*.

*Blazing Saddles* played every hamlet in America that was big enough to have a Bijou or a Roxy. It became one of those pictures that seems to go on forever, giving a needed boost to every drive-in owner faced with a long weekend and no new flick to bring them in.

The public loved *Blazing Saddles* and the kind of insanity that had Count Basie's band wailing in the middle of the Palmdale Desert. This time, the critics gave Brooks their full attention. Canby, as usual, spent most of his review talking about Woody Allen. But *Time* magazine was unreserved in its praise. As usual, many critics believed the film to be only accidentally good. This time Brooks went into a rage. With his film an acknowledged hit, reviewers still refused to give him credit. They insisted he didn't know what he was doing. Part of the difficulty was that some critics still did not fully appreciate or understand Brooks's style. They thought that because they were confused, Brooks was confused. He wasn't. Every minute of screen time in *Blazing Saddles* was carefully planned, from the moment the black sheriff arrives in town with his Gucci saddle bags, to an anguished citizen complaining "People are being stampeded and the cattle raped," to the preacher who lifts up his eyes to heaven and says, "Oh Lord! Can we accomplish this great feat in one night? Or are we just . . . jerking off?"

With its racial epithets and four-letter words, *Blazing Saddles* outraged the sensibilities of a number of critics and viewers. But, as Peter Schjeldahl wrote in *The New York Times*, *Blazing Saddles* is a movie "that some people are bound to despise; it wouldn't be for real if some people didn't despise it. Brooks is America's current patron saint of 'going too far,' a maniac yak-artist in the checkered tradition of burlesque, the Marx Brothers and *Mad* Magazine. A show-biz primitive, he specializes in the humor of affront— affront to civilized sensibilities, good taste and common sense—and makes us believe that he would do absolutely anything for a laugh."

Although Schjeldahl also insisted on comparing Brooks with Woody Allen, he was the first reviewer to admit that Brooks's style was a new invention. "In *The Producers* and now in *Blazing Saddles*, Brooks has brought to the screen a brand of convulsive comedy so completely original that it seems to have dropped out of the sky. Whatever else he may be, Brooks is unique and irreplaceable; let us cherish him for that."

Brooks by this time was considered a connoisseur of bad taste. He seldom allowed this

criticism to bother him. But one unfortunate mis-
understanding showed him to be a man not only
of taste but sensitivity. In *Blazing Saddles*, Alex
Karras plays a homicidal giant named Mongo who
is scolded by a citizen on horseback for illegally
parking his Brahma bull. Mongo hulks over and
knocks out the citizen's horse with one punch.

On March 31, 1974, *The New York Times*
published a letter in which a reader named Terry
Boyle protested the sequence: "As a parent of a
retarded child, I found myself appalled at the return of the 'village idiot' as a source of humor"
in *Blazing Saddles*. The letter continued, "From
the point of view of every organization and every
parent who has worked for the acceptance of
Mongoloid children and all retarded children in
the community, Mel Brooks has committed a
grievous offense against humanity." The letter was
reprinted in *Mental Retardation News*.

Brooks was stunned. He replied immediately to
the editors of *Mental Retardation News*. He was
distressed that anyone could believe that the
"writers of *Blazing Saddles* would be as cruel,
heartless and unthinking as to allude comically to
anyone suffering from Down's Syndrome in a film
scenario. . . ."

Brooks in no way tried to defend his position,
or to imply that Mr. Boyle did not appreciate his
humor. But he took the trouble to explain the
development of the character sketch in his letter.
"To begin with, the character's name in *Blazing
Saddles* is not, and has never been, 'Mongol.' The
character's name is 'Mongo,' and that name was
created only for the joke which occurs when the
man in the serape sees him entering town. The
man says, 'Mongo . . . Santa Maria'; and if you're

a fan of good jazz music, I'm sure you well know, as I do, that Mongo Santa Maria is one of the greatest bongo players that ever lived. The name Mongo was a tribute to him.

"The character was based on Hoss (the late Dan Blocker), who used his great strength to help, rather than hurt men, and we felt that Alex Karras was a good, strong choice to play him; and in the end he helped Mongo to become one of the most entertaining and beloved characters in the film.

"I have spoken to everyone connected with *Blazing Saddles* about Terry Boyle's letter and have shown them the mail that has come in from the parents of children suffering from Down's Syndrome. I cannot tell you how truly heartsick everyone connected with the film feels.

"One of the joys in making comedy films is the thrill I get when I hear the laughter in a darkened theater and know that I have made people happy. I must tell you in all candor, reading that letter and the endorsement of it in the *Mental Retardation News* was one of the unhappiest moments of my life."

This criticism had sickened Brooks. But the part of *Blazing Saddles* which evoked more critical reaction than any other—the farting scene—made him defiant. Considered the most vulgar piece of comedy ever seen on the screen, the world seemed to demand an explanation from Brooks. The point of the farts, said Melvin, were the farts.

Along with recognition as a comic entity separate from all standards of accepted form, *Blazing Saddles* also clearly identified Brooks as a writer-director whose work was in the genre of bad taste. Cries of protest fell upon his head. The farting scene triggered columns of speculation in the national press. Academic essayists devoted themselves to the subject. What was bad taste? Did it serve any purpose? Was it funny? Brooks was surprised that what he considered merely funny had created a major controversy around the country. He told reporters that he and the other writers simply thought the scene was amusing. He said when he was a kid, a fart was a guaranteed laugh-getter. But he had never seen one in the movies. In all those Westerns where characters consumed beans both day and night he could never understand why they didn't fart. That was all there was to it.

The controversy seemed to grow instead of diminish. If Brooks thought the scene was funny, did anyone else? Or did audiences just laugh out of embarrassment? Was the quality of an embarrassed laugh equal to a laugh of enjoyment? The writers didn't seem to know. A laugh was a laugh. Brooks gave it more thought, and came up with an interesting validation of the scene: Bad taste does indeed serve a purpose. It points out certain absurdities which exist in good taste. For instance, it is usual to see brutality in films. Violence is common on the screen. Murder and rape are gratuitous. Few people are concerned except when the murder is exceptionally gory. But a clean-cut blood-letting, in war films for example, raises few to outrage. Why, then, should anyone be shocked by a harmless fart? Farting, in the critical view, was a clean-cut form of vulgarity. If clean-cut violence was acceptable, why not clean-cut vulgarity?

*Blazing Saddles* actually qualified for a PG rating (Parental Guidance recommended), because there is no specific nudity and the language is not in the extreme. Brooks requested an R rating for *Blazing Saddles* because he wanted the public, especially parents who might think their children were going to see a cowboy movie, to be warned that the film contained sequences and language that might be considered vulgar.

Thus he was indignant when people complained that he used foul language, claiming that he had recommended caution. Some people felt Brooks was going for cheap laughs when he used swear words so frequently in the movie, especially "shit." Brooks answered he has nothing against cheap jokes, if they're funny. Words like "shit" loosen up an audience, he believes, and when he unleashes an unexpected phrase like "jerking off" it gets a howl.

*Blazing Saddles*, like Brooks's two earlier films, was notable for its pubescent approach to sex. Cinematically, Brooks's view of sex is like that of a twelve-year-old boy peering through the window of a lady's boudoir or an old-man drooling over a teenage Lolita. "Juvenile" is the word most often associated with Brooks when it comes to women.

In *The Producers* he introduced a lush blond secretary as an "adult educational toy"—she can't speak English, can't type, and can't take short-hand. When Zero Mostel tells her to go to work, she begins to dance like a demented, big-breasted Barbie Doll. In *Blazing Saddles* the moronic governor, played by Brooks, is so busy lusting after an oversized half-naked dance hall beauty that he can't be bothered to talk about business.

On the subject of sex, Brooks appears blatantly outspoken. He likes his sex low down and dirty, he tells reporters whenever they ask, which is often. Romance doesn't interest him. Just give him a crummy hotel room and a big-boobed broad who knows the ropes, and he's happy.

The truth is that Mel Brooks is a highly moral man who in many ways is old-fashioned in his regard for women. The rambunctious quality of his sexual film sequences can be attributed to two factors: He would be embarrassed to treat sex romantically in a movie; and the drooling chase around the desk is a standard comedic device—people are funny when they are chasing each other around.

But for the slapstick sexual scenes in *Blazing Saddles*, he selected one of the most sophisticated comediennes on the screen—Madeline Kahn. "Mel is sensual with me," says Kahn. "He treats me like an uncle—a dirty uncle. He's always hugging me, making dirty little remarks, but nice. He's an earthy man and very moral underneath. He has traditional values."

Brooks is a sophisticated man, although he does everything he can to obscure this fact. While certain characters in his films—characters that he makes look foolish—may have a chauvinistic approach to women, Brooks himself seems to judge people for themselves. He respects independence in either sex.

While he is a devoted family man in the traditional sense, he also is a man who has a strong personal identity. He does not use his wife and children to define his own personality. He knows who he is—crazy Mel Brooks, Man of a Thousand Faces. He's the forever kid—sensitive, intuitive, kind, generous, overpowering, energetic, sweet, powerful, and childlike. He is a comedic genius. He is literate and accomplished, but a rough-cut diamond, at home on the streets of Brooklyn or in the Waldorf Towers. His talent is so dazzling that he is one of the few people ever to successfully write, direct, and perform in such diverse media as stage, television, film, recordings, and advertising. A man of such enormous gifts and insights could never leave one entire area of his life— women—undeveloped and unexplored. Or, to put it another way, and more concisely: If Mel Brooks were a chauvinist, he would not be married to Anne Bancroft.

# 9

# The Marriage

"I have a great wife," he said, "Anne Bancroft —you've heard of her—who's my friend as well as my wife in a clinical way." He jokes about Bancroft's fame, but it is a joke that hides an immense pride, not so much of her but of himself, because he's the man whom such an "illustrious" woman chose to marry.

On one famous David Susskind show where several Jewish men, including Brooks and David Steinberg, talked about their mothers, Susskind commented that Jewish men traditionally made the best husbands because they were such good providers. He described the mink coats, Lincoln Continentals, and other trinkets Jewish husbands were expected to buy for their wives. Asked if he agreed, Brooks said: "Not me. Why should I buy? Annie makes a hundred a week." The allusion of course was that Anne Bancroft can probably buy and sell half of New York City, and Mel Brooks thinks that's fabulous. One of the richest women in the world loves *him*.

Although friends of both predicted their marriage would last three months, the Brooks-Bancroft merger has proved a strong and lasting union. "Annie and Mel are as well mated as any couple I've ever seen," says Carl Reiner. "They both are sharp and bright and volatile—quick to anger, quick to forgive."

As Bancroft says, "If we didn't enjoy the same kind of humor, we'd both be in jail. It's lovely, our relationship, and I wish it to every woman in the world."

Of course there are occasional battles. Anne likes to bait Mel, looking for some funny and outrageous new line. In one legendary argument, Mel said something about Anne's body. "My body!" she cried. "Don't you know my body's my instrument!" "Oh, yeah," sneered Mel. "Then let's hear you play 'Begin the Beguine.' "

"Deep down we're very much the same . . . we believe in the same things. Sometimes he'll be funny when I'm trying to be serious, but many times he doesn't even know when he's being really hilarious . . . usually when he's trying to be serious."

Heralded for years as a "true artist" who cared nothing for glamor, Bancroft had filled out yet another dimension of her career when Mike Nichols cast her in *The Graduate*. In the featured role of Mrs. Robinson, she claimed the movie for her own. A whole new range immediately was added to her personality. The public and critics had to reconsider her all over again. In 1970, she won an Emmy for her television special called *Annie: The Women in the Life of a Man*, produced by Martin Charnin.

Bancroft's glamorous image in *The Graduate* and the television show was so strong that it's difficult nowadays to think of her rough-hewn beginnings. But when the "new" glamor-girl was asked how she liked being an internationally known star, she replied: "I don't like it very much. If I could be famous by name and not with my face, I'd like it a lot better. Sometimes it's really bad . . . when you're rushing around with things to do . . . 'I gotta buy those lamb chops, I gotta cook' . . . and there are people in the supermarket, talking away to you."

Frank Langella was a relative unknown when he starred opposite Bancroft in William Gibson's *Cry of Players*. Langella comments: "I love her. As an actress, she has an infallible sense of truth and on stage she's infallible. It is impossible for that woman to do an unreal thing. Very few actresses of her stature and ability would have worked in a play that is not a vehicle for her— especially after *The Graduate*. Do you know she still gets letters from Mrs. Robinsons all over the country who say young boys call them up in the middle of the night? One Mrs. Robinson wrote that she got a call from a young boy who said, 'Boy, have I got a diploma for you.' "

Like Brooks, Anne is, and then again is not, an advocate of women's liberation. Several years ago she was asked if she disliked men opening doors and lighting cigarettes for her. She said, "Don't be silly, I love it. What I resent is the assumption that if they do those things, they have fulfilled their responsibility. It's easy to do all the little polite things, but not face up to real responsibilities as a man to a woman."

She laughed when a *Women's Wear Daily* reporter reminded her of the quote. "My God, I was magnificent there, wasn't I? I was so smart before I was married . . . but I think I still believe that. I do believe women are weaker . . . no, I don't like that word 'weaker' . . . but we succumb more to our emotions. Because men aren't so emotional, their intellects are usually intact. They owe that to us, and we owe them other things . . . the things we can do that they can't . . . like crying for them sometimes."

Anne claimed in 1970 that she never heard of N.O.W. and thought that feminist organizations were slightly ridiculous. Like many highly successful women, Bancroft insisted that she was an "old-fashioned woman." She had a tendency to cover up the aggressive side of her character.

Today, Bancroft acknowledges her feminist feelings as well as her forcefulness. But she remains a strong supporter of the male sex. She thinks men are in greater need of equality. "So much is expected from them . . . I will join any movement to help them. We must make life less difficult for men. They are so oppressed. Men are getting the worst of all worlds."

The birth of their child, Maximilian Michael, in June of 1972, caused Brooks and Bancroft to reconsider their lifestyle.

"There are difficulties when there are two careers in one family," said Anne, "and now with the baby we have agreed that we can't make our films at the same time." There is no doubt in her mind which comes first, career or family. The life of an internationally known actress is a demanding one. Film productions are located all over the world. And Bancroft has determined that she will make no further films abroad.

"Mel's the man in our family," Anne continued, "and an example to our son, and someone had to give in. Besides, I have to be where Mel can reach me easily, if he cannot come with me."

Currently Bancroft limits herself to one big project a year. "When I do commit, I commit myself heart and soul. I'm always lonely when I work. You're going through a very private inner experience that requires personal strength. I accept this loneliness, but it's one of the big fears of going back to work."

Whenever there is an important event in Brooks's life, his wife is at his side. This is no less true for her. Brooks has tremendous respect for his wife's career. He views Anne as his wife, and Bancroft as one of the world's finest actresses. Accordingly, he treats each of them with enormous consideration and admiration. They try to work on their projects at different times of the year so that if one must travel the whole family can go along.

If Brooks must go on a promotional tour, Bancroft almost always accompanies him. When she is on location, you can look for him. For the most part, Bancroft has given up foreign location shooting because she is not easily available if there is an emergency at home.

"We have always done what we wanted to do," says Bancroft, "never anything chic or popular. Every job we have ever done is because we have wanted to, which is why we're happy."

Both Mel and Anne were dedicated New Yorkers. For years they swore they would never live anywhere else. One special reason for remaining in New York was so that Mel could see his three children by his first marriage on a regular basis. Brooks always said he would like to have twice as many children as the four he has fathered. Why? "It's the right number to carry your coffin when you die from the heart attack which having eight children will certainly give you."

He is devoted to all of his children. Stefanie, now eighteen, studies at Brandeis University. She is "very smart, brilliant. She should be a writer." Nicholas, seventeen, "should be a doctor or a film-maker." And Edward, sixteen, "should go into film or theater."

When the children were old enough to be on their own, Brooks heeded the call to move to the West Coast. Both careers demanded more and more time in Hollywood.

How did two such intrepid city dwellers survive the transition from sidewalk to grass? Years earlier, Bancroft told Louella Parsons, "It really doesn't matter where you live. What matters is who you live with." But Brooks—still frightened of airplanes—manages to fly across the country at least twice a month to see his children.

Nothing could better illustrate Brooks's point of view regarding women than his participation in the children's book and television special *Free to Be . . . You and Me*. *Free to Be*, as every child in the country knows by now, was born of a concept by Marlo Thomas. In a search for reading material for her niece, Miss Thomas found most available literature dull—and sexist as well. "In the books," she said, "boys invent things and girls use them. That kind of a thing is a putdown of the human race." As a result, she asked dozens of her friends in the publishing and entertainment business to help her put together a book from which they made a television special and a record. *Free to Be* was, according to Marlo Thomas, "the celebration of the self, the idea that a child should feel, 'It's terrific to be me; I'm unique.' "

The program encouraged children to be themselves—both in what they did and what they felt. Girls were depicted as athletic and mechanical and boys were encouraged to play with dolls and cry. Former football star Roosevelt Grier sang, "It's all right to cry, crying gets the sad out of you."

Carl Reiner and Peter Stone wrote a cartoon sketch about two newborn babies. The film sequence was animated with voiceovers for the babies. Who better to play a baby than gravelly voiced Mel Brooks? Marlo Thomas played the other infant. Together the two tots explore themselves and each other on their first morning in the world.

HIGH VOICE: What do you think I am?

DEEP VOICE: You? That's easy—you're a boy.

HIGH VOICE: Are you sure?

DEEP VOICE: Of course I'm sure. I'm alive already four, five minutes, and I haven't been wrong yet.

The deep voice insists it's a girl: "Cute feet. Small, dainty. Yup, yup, I'm a girl."

Brooks was becoming increasingly popular as a personality. One week, in December 1973, radio station WBAI, a noncommercial, *avant garde* New York station, was airing a five-day nonstop reading of *War and Peace* by such celebrities as Dustin Hoffman, Anne Bancroft, Stacy Keach, Tony Randall, Rip Torn, and 142 other famous names in theater and literature. Listeners called in at all hours of the day and night to find out when a particular reader would be broadcasting.

The one reader most people asked to hear was none other than "your obedient Jew," Mel Brooks.

Brooks was aware of a growing band of Mel Brooks loyalists or cultists, as film reviewers like to call them, but these people were not bombarding him with mail. "The true cultists" he said, "are very bright and very shy at the same time and they do not write letters to you." Anne Bancroft, conscious of her husband's growing popularity, remarked, "He's always been funny, professionally and privately," she says. "He's always been acclaimed, it's just that the circle of admirers is getting wider and wider."

In 1973, Warner Brothers Records reissued the three *2000-Year-Old Man* records, together with a new album called *2000 and Thirteen*. One side of *2000 and Thirteen* was new material, especially recorded for this album, but the other side was made up of what Brooks called "the Dead Sea Scrolls." These were tapes from all the parties at which he and Reiner did their stuff for free during the 1950s. These tapes, like certain recordings of Lenny Bruce or unissued rock performances, have enjoyed a demand circulation for twenty years among the sub-underground of Mel Brooks cultists. Shrewdly, Warner's decided that since just about everyone was now a cultist, the tapes should be made available to the general public.

It had been thirteen years since the release of the original album. Despite a severe case of nerves, Brooks and Reiner agreed to improvise new routines before a live audience made up of about two hundred of their friends. Guests made themselves comfortable in the huge sofas set up in Warner's Burbank studio and were served cracked crab and chili from Chasen's. There were old friends such as Arthur Penn and producer Norman Lear. Pre-performance jitters started a rumor that Brooks and Reiner had decided at the last minute to skip it. "He hasn't been very easy to live with this week," Bancroft commented. Reiner, like Brooks, had become enormously successful as a television and film writer, director, and producer over the previous ten years. Both Reiner and Brooks now said that the need to perform was past.

But after a short delay, the team appeared. For the next hour and a half the audience watched a chain-smoking and initially rusty Brooks settle into the character of the ancient Jew.

Reiner had said, "Mel is at his best when he's up against the wall and doesn't know which way he's going to go." Reiner's specialty was pushing Brooks from one brick wall to another. Brooks would lope along making apparent sense until Reiner pushed him just a little bit too far, then Mel would flash on something completely insane. That was the approach Reiner took now, heightening the humor with his eager-beaver and ingenuous tone.

"Who was the best dancer you ever saw?" he asked Brooks.

The best dancer in all of history, claimed Mel, was Abraham Lincoln. "He used to lock the door and jump and twirl in graceful arabesques. But he never went on the stage because of his warts."

"What was the greatest medical discovery in your 2000 years?"

"Liquid Prell," came the quick reply. "A heart-lung machine is in your medicine chest," he explained. "It falls out, and it breaks. But entire families are being held together by liquid Prell."

What percent of your four or five hundred marriages would you say were successful?"

"Seventy-one percent. The rest were squabbles, 'Don't eat your soup with your fork.' "

Once started, it was like the old days. "It was like the return of Jenny Lind," said Reiner in the glow of the post-performance flow of congratulations. "I'm glad I was born during Mel Brooks's lifetime," said one fan.

"I'm glad I'm in Los Angeles this week, but that's going too far," retorted writer Nora Ephron.

Brooks and Reiner were exhilarated by the recording session. "We only needed fifteen minutes," said Brooks. "And I think we got it all."

*The New York Times* greeted the new album with enthusiasm: "How important can Spiro Agnew seem when we are listening to a guy who bought a cabinet from Jesus and fooled around with Dolly Madison? What kind of medical discovery is a heart-lung machine compared to liquid Prell? . . . Like Chaplin's tramp or Harpo's mute, the bimillenarian portrayed by Brooks and interviewed by Reiner is a comedy classic all the more dazzling because of its improvisational nature. The humor centers on the improbable paths Brooks's mind takes him in response to the seemingly innocent and sane questions from Reiner. . . . Naturally there is a New York ethnic quality inherent in the 2013-Year-Old Man, but that is only one level of an appeal that is truly universal."

Fifteen other comedy albums were released at the same time as *2000 and Thirteen*. Against such hit comedy performers as George Carlin and David Steinberg, Brooks and Reiner not only stood up, but shone.

# 10

## Brooks Meets Frankenstein

Gene Wilder had been a last-minute replacement as the Waco Kid in *Blazing Saddles*. When a veteran actor originally signed for the part cancelled out, Wilder, as a favor to Brooks, caught the first plane from New York and did the role. To return the favor, Brooks agreed to direct a screenplay Wilder was working on called *Young Frankenstein*.

After Wilder's first draft, Brooks collaborated on the revision. Isolated in a room at the Bel Air Hotel, Brooks and Wilder wrote the final screenplay. *Young Frankenstein* was intended as a parody of and a tribute to all the great monster movies of the Thirties. The writers created a film to play on two levels. One, to make a hilarious satire of the old black-and-white horror films, and second, to offer reverent homage to those same beautifully made movies. The story was as old as Mary Shelley's book and as intriguing as James Whale's 1930 film *Frankenstein*. Wilder and Brooks saw no reason to change it. What they felt was important was to develop the characterizations—people who would make the tale of pride and horror live as the funniest movie since *Blazing Saddles.*

It was a productive collaboration. "My job was to make him more subtle," said Wilder. "His job was to make me more broad. I would say, 'I don't want this to be *Blazing Frankenstein*,' and he'd answer, 'I don't want an art film that only fourteen people see.' " Wilder proved an excellent alter ego for Brooks and the combination has been one of the most creative partnerships in Brooks's career. Gene Wilder, who has been described by Herbert Gold as a "six-foot pink-eyed mouse," has a comic sense diametrically opposed to Brooks's hyper-extroverted style, although he says he has learned many of the rudiments of comedic acting from Brooks. "Mel will take a shotgun with fifty pellets in it," said Wilder. "Fifteen miss the target and another fifteen hit the outside rim. Ten more hit nearer to the center, and ten are right on the bulls-eye. I take a high-powered rifle, a steady aim, and try to hit the center. It may be a fault and it may be a virtue. I don't know. Mel will say: 'I want to be funny, funny.' Instead of a firecracker every seven seconds, I say 'I'd be very happy if we could let the explosion wait until I get some of the story told.' "

The writers wanted all the characters in *Young Frankenstein* to be motivated and three-dimensional. They created Freddy Frankenstein as a mild-mannered modern doctor with all his famous grandfather's ambition seething beneath the surface. He is driven by the conflict between his reasonable good sense and his desire to complete his grandfather's dream. Frau Blucher, the housekeeper, is motivated by the love she still feels for the dead Dr. Frankenstein. And the monster, for all his abnormal brain, is just an overgrown two-year-old discovering the world.

*Young Frankenstein* was a perfect vehicle for Brooks's sense of the absurd. It included such bits as the housekeeper leading young Frankenstein up to his castle bedchamber with an unlighted candelabrum, and a police inspector who wears a monocle over his eye patch.

Brooks even satisfied those who prefer their humor outrageous. In one scene, an innocent maiden observes that a large monster "would have a big *schwantzstucker*." And later the superendowed monster ghoul drives Freddy's fiancée, a self-described virgin, to what must be the groaningest screen orgasm ever.

When it came to casting the film, Brooks sought out his most trusted players as well as some new faces. Madeline Kahn was his choice to play Freddy's repressed, wild-haired fiancée, who eventually finds sexual fulfillment in the arms of the monster. Cloris Leachman as Frau Blucher, the housekeeper, played a witty parody of Judith Anderson in *Rebecca.* Marty Feldman was Igor, complete with a movable hump and askew eyes. Teri Garr, as Inga the laboratory assistant, recalled every blonde starlet who never made the big time. And as the monster, Brooks cast Peter Boyle. Boyle had special problems acting the part of the monster. He had no spoken lines and his extremely complicated makeup limited the range of facial expressions. But Boyle succeeded in creating an impression of a monster who is really a giant-sized child.

Other well-known actors who are not regulars often seek parts in Brooks's films for the pure fun of being in one, and the experience of working with Mel Brooks. Gene Hackman, perhaps the most sought-after actor in films today, called Brooks and asked if he could do the cameo role of the blind man in *Young Frankenstein*. Hackman was surprised when Brooks hesitated. Mel was slightly embarrassed. He knew that Hackman was a fine actor as well as a big star, but he didn't know if he could play comedy. He asked him if he would audition. Hackman agreed. Brooks put him through an audition similar to the grueling exercise he asked of Madeline Kahn on her first Brooks film. Brooks at once recognized that Hackman would be brilliant in the comedy role. Hackman expected the scene to take two or three hours to shoot. Instead, it took four days, from six in the morning till nine every night. From those four days came four golden minutes of classic screen comedy.

All of Brooks's players must pass two acid tests. They are chosen for their talent and their lack of neurosis. With the notable exception of Zero Mostel, Brooks has avoided duplicating the working conditions that gave everyone ulcers on *Your Show of Shows*. Brooks acknowledges that Mostel is a comedic genius, but genius is hard to work into a stock company. Mostel, says Herbert Gold, is something like an Orson Welles of comedy— not made for group development of a product. Brooks does not surround himself with large egos who compete with one another to see who can be funniest and craziest. For all the talk about those golden years in television, Brooks obviously doesn't miss them enough to recreate them in his own staff.

On the set of *Young Frankenstein*, Brooks worked easily with his carefully picked company.

He appeared carefree and one-hundred percent positive that this picture would be a hit. In an effort to quit smoking, he chewed endless sticks of Trident cinnamon gum as well as eating an ongoing stream of Raisinettes. Brooks seldom stopped performing. Directing a gag, he would often crumple to the floor and lie there clutching his sides with laughter. Between takes he would lurch into an imaginary swordfight with Wilder, usually followed by an imitation of Gene Kelly's *Singing in the Rain* dance sequence, crying at the top of his voice, "Fellini and Dick Lester are great directors, but are they tops in taps?"

Peter Boyle enjoyed watching Brooks so much that he even showed up on the set when he had a day off. Boyle described Brooks's directing style as "controlled madness." But Madeline Kahn said, "Mel is not an easy-going, lax, casual person. He's very energetic and intense."

Said Gene Wilder: "He has actors that know how to turn on their own motors, but he's a wonderful chauffeur. He has trouble when an actor can't start himself. He'll perform something the way he wants it done and we'll laugh, but it won't work. That's why he keeps using the same people—we're all self-starters."

"Mel will shoot a take," adds Madeline Kahn, "then he'll say, 'we're gonna' do another and this time go bananas.' "

The members of the Mel Brooks Repertory Company, as it is informally known, know how to go crazy in the right places—in front of the cameras—and how to turn it off when Brooks says, "Cut!" This extraordinary control makes the regulars as well as the carefully selected non-regulars rare jewels. And Brooks hangs on to the jewels he finds. Although he still reserves the right to be "the only psychotic on the set," Brooks himself has calmed down considerably. He is neither as serious nor as crazy as he was in his Caesar show days. He has, in a word, mellowed. He obviously knows what he's doing now, and while the pressure of risking someone else's several million dollars still remains, there is the added assurance that he knows how to make films.

There was much affection among the cast and crew on the set of *Young Frankenstein*, as well as a love for the film itself. They wanted to make a picture that would show how real people would act if they were plunked down in Transylvania.

Near the end of the shooting schedule, Wilder, with tears standing in his eyes, said to Brooks, "I don't want to leave Transylvania. I've been so happy here."

The film seemed to have a charmed life. After *Young Frankenstein* was in the can, Brooks edited the picture frame by frame at least twelve times, and in the last week of production spent several hours in a recording room, gleefully snorting, grunting, snarling, groaning, sighing, and guffawing to fill tiny gaps in the talk track. "The man is a demon," said one of his editors. "Nothing less than greatness will satisfy him. He has a passion for perfection."

Unlike his temper tantrums over interference during the filming of *The Producers*, Brooks was anxious to show off scenes from *Young Frankenstein*. He often invited interviewers and even critics to watch him edit the film. Brooks insisted that Wilder also participate in the editing. When Wilder asked why, Brooks said "just pay attention." Much of the editing was done in a small theater. On one typical editing day, Brooks and his collaborators worked on a scene in which Gene Hackman as the blind hermit is visited by the monster. Hackman answers the door, obviously pleased to have company. "What is your name?" Hackman asks the monster. There are a few slightly muffled growls. "I didn't get that," says Hackman, looking momentarily puzzled before continuing his enthusiastic welcome. Hackman then blindly offers the monster a cigar and carefully lights his thumb.

Hackman questioned the timing of the scene, but Brooks was lost in admiration for his work. They debated the possibility of cutting a shot that particularly pleased Brooks. "The only thing I hate to give up is my applause from the *Cinematographers Journal*, but," Brooks sighed before continuing, "I'll give it up for a laugh." The shot was eliminated.

A shot of the monster walking down a cobblestone street was also eliminated. Brooks had gone all the way over to MGM to find the right cobblestone street, and it broke his heart to take the scene out.

Modest to the end, Brooks watched one of his favorite scenes. "That's one of the greatest scenes ever done on film, and it has some of my best, prettiest photography." Still sensitive to criticism that he has no film technique, Brooks applied himself to making *Young Frankenstein* a technical achievement. He filmed in black and white because he felt he couldn't properly satirize as well as salute the 1930s style of horror film if he used color. He was unruffled by Andy Warhol's version of Frankenstein which was due to be released at the same time. Warhol's film was high camp, while Brooks was dedicated to preserving the style of the traditional horror movies—from his own hilarious viewpoint. His was a modern film taking place in contemporary times, but he used old-style wipes and iris shots, retaining the feeling of the great horror films of the Thirties and Forties. The love scenes in *Young Frankenstein* were so "old Hollywood," that they ended with closeups of logs blazing up suddenly in the fireplace.

*Young Frankenstein* closely follows the original story. It begins with the will of Dr. Victor Frankenstein being transported to New York, where it is presented to his grandson, Freddy (Gene Wilder), a surgeon and lecturer on neurosurgery. Soon he is on his way to Transylvania, where he will claim the ancestral estate. Every story point is accompanied by flashes of lightning and loud rolls of thunder.

In one early scene, Freddy Frankenstein is on his way to visit his grandfather's castle for the first time. He has gone at the urging of family friend Herr Falkstein. As his train pulls into the station, Freddy throws open the window and sticks his head out. Brooks starts his usual musical parody, this time it's *Chattanooga Choo-Choo*. Freddy says "Pardon me, boy, is this the Transylvania Station?" The boy tells Freddy it is, and that he's on track 29. The boy starts walking off, then suddenly turns around and asks Freddy if he wants a shine. The train pulls to a stop and Freddy gets off. A crack of lightning illuminates a small, cloaked figure with large, strange eyes that are constantly looking in different directions. Freddy introduces himself, insisting his name is pronounced "Fron-kon-steen," then notices that the man is a hunchback. Freddy asks if he is Igor.

Igor says it's pronounced "Eye-gor." And he tells Freddy that his grandfather, Herr Falkstein, thought it would be ironically appropriate if he worked for Freddy. But of course, he says, the rates have gone up. Freddy agrees and assures Igor that they'll get on splendidly together. In his uneasiness, Freddy slaps Igor on his hump. He apologizes profusely, telling Igor that he didn't mean to embarrass him in any way. Freddy also tells him that he's a brilliant surgeon, and suggests that he could help Igor with his hump. Igor looks straight at Freddy with his immense eyes, and asks, "What hump?"

Igor climbs into the driver's seat of a horse-drawn cart, telling Freddy that he'll be more comfortable in the rear. As Freddy throws his suitcase into the cart, a woman's voice screams in pain. "What was that?" Freddy asks. Igor tells him that it's Inga, the laboratory assistant. Freddy peers into the cart and sees the very large-breasted Inga lying on a bale of hay. Would Freddy like to roll in the hay? Inga inquires. It's lots of fun, she sings. "Roll, roll . . . roll in the hay; roll, roll . . . roll in the hay." Igor cracks the whip and the horses start off as Freddy scurries into the cart with a happy grin on his face.

The scene dissolves to the old castle. It's nighttime and stormy, naturally. On a distant hill we see the original Frankenstein castle. As the cart reaches the gigantic tower, Igor steps down and approaches. The huge door is illuminated by a torch in an iron sconce on each side. He grasps two enormous wrought-iron knockers and raps them against the door. The sound echoes through the castle. Freddy watches in amazement as he helps Inga down from the cart. "What knockers!"

he comments, staring at the castle door. Inga, rather shyly, says "Thanks."

The massive door slowly creaks open and a woman appears. She announces that her name is Frau Blucher. At the sound of her name, a bolt of lightning flashes across the sky.

The group disappears into the castle and the scene dissolves to Victor Frankenstein's famous library. Having stumbled upon his grandfather's secret library, Freddy sees a large book lying on the table. A crack of lightning lights up the room and the book's title becomes clearly visible: *How I Did It*, by Victor Frankenstein. Seeing the title, Igor comments that it's a good name. He says "How To" books are always good sellers.

As Freddy opens to the first page of the book, a low rumble of thunder is heard in the background. Disbelieving and amused, Freddy begins to read the first page aloud: "Whence, I often asked myself, did the principles of life proceed? To examine the causes of life . . . we must first have recourse to death."

"What a fruitcake!" Freddy says of his grandfather. "He must have been a real nut." In a mocking voice, Freddy continues: "And as soon as the dazzling light vanished, the oak tree had disappeared, I knew then that electricity and galvanism had changed my life." Freddy interrupts his reading and comments on grandfather's insanity again, then resumes reading: "When I look back now, it seems to me as if this almost miraculous event obliterated any last effort to avert the storm that was even then hanging in the stars."

By now, Freddy is howling with laughter as he continues to read out loud: "Change the poles from plus to minus and from minus to plus! I alone succeeded in discovering the cause of generation of life. Nay, even more—I, myself, became capable of bestowing animation upon lifeless matter." Freddy is by this time on the floor.

But Freddy decides to follow in his grandfather's footsteps. Gene Wilder plays Freddy straight, but little by little the essential madness begins to come out. He cannot resist the temptation to create an ideal person. He and Igor decide to snatch a body from a graveyard and to implant in it a very special brain.

It's a gray night. The rain falls incessantly. The whole movie is gray, black, and silver. The camera pulls back to reveal a prison graveyard. A freshly executed body can be seen swinging back and forth, a black hood covering its head. Two gravediggers and a guard stand looking up at the body. Brooks swings back into musical parody as one gravedigger says to the other, "He's swinging in the rain." The guard cuffs the second gravedigger as the scene immediately dissolves to Freddy and Igor knee-deep in the grave, shoveling dirt. Freddy complains that they are doing a filthy job. Igor says it could be worse, it could start raining harder. As he says it, a crack of thunder sounds and a torrential downpour follows. Freddy turns and stares at Igor.

Back in the laboratory, Freddy and Igor put the body on an operating table and cover it with a sheet. Freddy marvels at the perfect body, and notes that all they need now is an equally magnificent brain. As he prepares a hypodermic, he asks Igor if he has the name that he wrote down. Igor grins wickedly, looks at the name inked on the palm of his hand, and reads "Dr. H. Delbruck."

Freddy insists, "I must have that brain, and

only that brain. Delbruck was the finest natural philosopher, internal diagnostician, and chemical therapist of this century." Igor wonders out loud how Delbruck died. Freddy lowers his head; "VD," he says.

Freddy is sure that Delbruck's brain can still function since he's only been dead for two weeks. He's sure the depository where the brain is being kept has preserved it well.

The scene dissolves to a partially open hospital door. On the upper half of the glass door is printed:

BRAIN DEPOSITORY
AFTER FIVE P.M., SLIP BRAINS
THROUGH SLOT IN DOOR

The shadow of a hunchbacked man holding a lantern is silhouetted from inside the depository.

Inside the darkened depository the sounds of low thunder can be heard. A row of brains in jars, under domes, rests on a long, narrow table. Igor tiptoes slowly, examining the labels on each glass dome. "Albertus Magnus (Physicist)," "Cornelius Agrippa (Natural Philosopher)," "Lawrence Talbot (Hematologist)." Then he comes to: "Hans Delbruck (Scientist and Saint)." Igor lifts off the glass dome and takes the jar containing the brain of Hans Delbruck. As he turns to leave, he sees himself in a full-length mirror. He drops the jar in fright. He looks down at the mess of brain and glass on the floor. He looks at the audience, and, with a shrug, says: "I tried!" Igor grabs another jar from under the nearest glass dome and leaves. On the empty dome is printed: "Do not use this brain! Abnormal."

An electrical storm is building in the distance.

Pointed toward the sky, the camera now travels down through a small opening at the top of the laboratory's ceiling. As it continues down, we hear electricity sparking, centrifuges whirring, wheels buzzing, chemicals bubbling in beakers.

The camera drifts past the archaic scientific equipment and comes to rest on a giant pair of shoes with iron soles. Slowly it reveals two enormous legs held down by leather straps to the operating table. The giant torso is similarly strapped. At last we see for the first time the creature's face. There are stitches across his neck and stitches circling the crown of his skull where a new brain has been inserted.

The camera pulls back to reveal Freddy and Inga. Freddy is wearing a long white surgeon's gown and mask. Inga says their new creation looks hideous. But to Freddy he is beautiful. He admires the creature with pride and feels a strong sense of ownership. He orders Igor first to check the generator, then to check the dials of a "battery indicator," which is connected to the creature's head. Inga watches Freddy admiringly. She tells him that he's not only a great doctor, but also a . . . As she tries to find the right word, Freddy supplies it! A GOD!

Thunder sounds again as the laboratory becomes an electrical circus. Igor throws the first switch, then the second switch and, finally, a switch marked "The Works." As the lights return to normal, black wisps of smoke rise from the creature's body. Freddy, soaked to the skin, places a stethoscope on the creature's heart and listens, but can't hear anything. He's crushed.

Freddy attempts to keep up the morale of his colleagues. He tells them that if science teaches people anything, it teaches them to accept failure as well as success, and to do it with quiet dignity and grace. Freddy looks once more, sadly, at the lifeless body, then grasps it by the throat, begins shaking it, and screams, "Son of a bitch bastard—what did you do to me?" Inga and Igor scream for Freddy to stop before he kills the lifeless creature, and they drag Freddy off.

Later that same night, Freddy, Igor, and Inga are in the dining room when they hear a strange moaning sound coming from the laboratory. The trio bursts into the lab to see the monster straining tentatively against the straps. His head is raised and he emits a loud, but pitiful, humming sound: "MMMMMMMMmmmmmmmmmmmmm." Freddy and his colleagues are ecstatic. They congratulate each other. They have defeated death!

The cautious Igor warns Freddy not to get too close because the monster could kill him. Freddy directs Inga to prepare a sedative just in case. Inga prepares the hypodermic. The monster raises his head and makes little circles with his hands, asking to be "free." Freddy feels sorry for his creation. It wants to talk, he says. It wants to take off the straps, and it wants to be free. Igor says he doesn't care what "it wants." They should consider what *they* want. Freddy tries to make Igor understand that the great brain of Hans Delbruck is inside the body pleading to be set free. Igor, who knows the brain is certainly not Delbruck's, says it's okay with him if they release the creature as long as they keep the body tied down.

Warning everyone to stand back, Freddy walks up to the creature and stands over him. The creature is silent, feeling his way. "Hello, there," says Freddy. The creature just hums. Feeling a little more confident, Freddy asks it how it's doing. The creature hums again in a tone that suggests "not so good." Putting on a pathetic expression, the creature starts crying softly. Freddy's heart goes out to the creature, and he says he's going to set it free. But just to be sure, Freddy asks Inga if the sedative is ready.

Freddy releases the strap across the monster's thighs and then unties the strap across his chest . . . and steps back. All eyes are on the monster. Tingly music. The monster looks at them for a moment while he is still lying down. A slightly sly grin comes to his mouth. He rises . . . slowly, carefully, to a sitting position, humming a low, suspicious groan.

Freddy holds out his hands reassuringly and asks it to give him its hands. The creature slowly extends both arms toward Freddy but looks as though it could either comply with Freddy's request or strangle him. Freddy takes the monster's hands and leads him in his first stiff steps.

Inga, frightened, backs away. Igor, with even more reason to be nervous, takes out a cigarette from his pocket and strikes a match. Terrified by the flame, the monster screams and grabs Freddy's throat. Freddy cries out for his colleagues to quickly give the monster something, but before he can say what, the monster squeezes his throat tighter, and Freddy can't make a sound. For a split second, the monster relaxes his grip, and Freddy again tries to tell them what he wants them to give the monster. Before he can finish, the monster again tightens his strangle hold, cutting Freddy off.

Freddy points desperately to the monster's arm. Igor asks if Freddy wants him to give the monster an arm. Freddy shakes his head no. He pushes his thumb against two fingers—miming an injection. Igor asks if he should give the monster a cigarette. Freddy shakes his head no and holds up three fingers. Suddenly it's charades, but Freddy is playing under a three-hundred-pound handicap.

Igor asks if there are three syllables. Freddy nods yes, holding up one finger for the first syllable. Freddy cups his hands for "sounds like," then points to his head. Inga guesses "head," and Freddy nods yes. Freddy is jubilant as Inga and Igor correctly guess "said." Freddy holds up two fingers for the second syllable, and mimes "tiny" with his fingers. After several unsuccessful attempts, Inga and Igor correctly guess "a."

Freddy cups his hands to his ears and mimes the word "give." Inga and Igor, thinking they now have it, guess "Said-a-give?" Freddy weakly shakes his head "no." Inga's eyes light up. She's got it. "Tive . . . Sedative!"

Freddy, who by now is practically dead, weakly points to his nose. Igor runs to the table and gets the hypodermic, then runs back and jams it into the monster's tush. The monster's eyes freeze. He looks at each of them, his hands still clutching Freddy's neck. Then he collapses like a giant tree.

Inga, rushing to the half conscious Freddy, asks him if he's all right. Freddy ignores her, turns to Igor and asks very sweetly if he can speak to him for a moment. Demonstrating extreme control, Freddy promises Igor that he won't be angry, but all he wants is the truth. Igor agrees. Freddy asks him if the brain that he brought back from the depository was that of Hans Delbruck. Igor says that in all honesty he has to say, "Not exactly."

Trying to hold back his rage, Freddy asks Igor

to be more specific. Igor says that if push came to shove, he would have to say no. Freddy promises Igor that he won't be angry, but exactly whose brain is it? Igor tells him that it was Abby someone. He thinks the full name was Abby Normal.

Realizing what has happened, Freddy explodes and lunges for Igor, screaming that he just put an abnormal brain into a seven-and-a-half-foot-long, forty-inch-wide gorilla! Igor, gasping as Freddy's hands tighten around his neck, yells out to Inga to quick, give him the . . . but Igor is interrupted by a loud knock. As Inga heads toward the door, Freddy releases Igor's neck and tells Igor to strap the monster down tightly.

As Freddy starts to leave, Igor asks him where he's going. Freddy tells him that he's going to wash up because they all have to look normal, and they all have to behave normally. At that moment, Freddy's clip-on bow tie unhinges from his collar and goes flying across the room.

The climax of the film is the sequence where Freddy takes his monster to a medical convention in Bucharest and demonstrates his accomplishment by joining the creature for several choruses of "Puttin' on the Ritz," both swankily dressed in white tie and tails.

Every once in a while, Brooks will still walk into a theater playing *Young Frankenstein*. It is one of the great thrills of his life to walk down the aisle and listen to the sound of laughter.

*Young Frankenstein* appears to be the ultimate outgrowth of all Brooks's years in comedy. And yet it bears little resemblance to any of his other work. The photography is magnificent. The story line is controlled. At bottom, the film deals with a theme which is of supreme importance to Brooks—the story of a man who challenges God by creating life. This is the reason that Brooks continues writing. Writing also creates life, and it goes on long after the writer has ceased to exist. It is a contribution. Brooks is a man who despises death.

"I don't want to make just another movie," he says. "I want to make trouble. I want to say in comic terms, '*J'accuse*.' We dealt with bigotry in *Saddles* and with neo-Fascism in *Producers*. Underneath the comedy in *Frankenstein*, the doctor is undertaking the quest to defeat death—to challenge God. Our monster lives, therefore he wants love too. He's really very touching in his lonely misery."

Brooks is serious about all this. But his cure for the poor fellow's isolation is to replace those lug bolts in his neck with a Courrèges zipper, and to have the heroine joyously discover that his "ol'" zipper neck is not his only monstrously proportioned part.

This time out, reviewers, although still divided, praised Brooks for his camera work and his fastidious attention to detail. Even Canby managed not to mention Woody Allen in his review. "As played by Gene Wilder in Mel Brooks's funniest, most cohesive comedy to date," Canby wrote for *The New York Times*, "this Dr. Frankenstein is a marvelous addled mixture of young Tom Edison, Winnie-the-Pooh and your average *Playboy* reader with a keen appreciation of beautiful bosoms."

Jay Cocks took up the Woody Allen theme for *Time* magazine, but this time considered Brooks "madder, funnier, more inspired than anything being done in movies today, including the rather coddled comedy of Woody Allen." But as usual, praise was often a facade for barbs. Cocks wrote: "As a comic and a film maker, Brooks wants to knock you cockeyed. For a laugh, he will do anything, try anything, he rains gags. After a Brooks bit, audiences can be exhausted; after a Brooks film, there is the lingering feeling of having been pummeled. Brooks is like a young, slightly skittish fighter whose energy compensates for lack of finesse. He hits out wildly, continuously, hoping that a few punches will land. Brooks generally succeeds. He keeps the pressure turned up high, and the laughs batter their way through. The attack is so relentless, it can leave the viewer bruised as well as amused."

Joy Boyum of the *World Sun Journal* was more direct: "Mel Brooks's *Young Frankenstein*, then, has to be something of a disappointment and primarily because too much of the humor is too predictable. And all of this is made to seem even more heavy handed by the overworking of many of its jokes.

"Still it's hard to deny Mel Brooks's comic gifts, however sporadically realized in this film's direction and script . . . for as with genre films and series, so with Mel Brooks: If you tried it and liked it, you'll probably try it and like it again."

Brooks knew he had come a long way when the intellectually pure, maliciously minded critic John Simon compared *Young Frankenstein* with other film comedies of 1975, including *Return of the Pink Panther*, *The Fortune*, and Woody Allen's *Love and Death*, going so far as to describe

Brooks's film as the best comedy of the year. Simon gave Brooks the privilege of intellectual analysis:

"It [Young Frankenstein] is a funny sendup of the horror film genre, first by spelling out absurd absurdities to which most of us have at one time or other paid emotional tribute; and secondly, by bringing to the surface things latent in the genre that have not dared to become conscious: the intense sexuality masquerading as horror, and the secret double identity of the only superficially monstrous monster as object of our lust as well as of our repressed empathy.

"I am not saying that a person who laughs loud at the film's jokes must be fully aware of these implications, but I do think that, consciously or unconsciously, the unifying undercurrent of hidden meanings made all but manifest helps make the laughter steadier and happier."

Brooks concurred that *Young Frankenstein* had a profound message. It is, he said, a picture about womb envy. What little boy wasn't upset when he first learned that he would never be able to make a baby? Freddy Frankenstein, discontent with the usual creative outlets open to men, wants to create life. And he succeeds. Behind every comic premise, Brooks feels there lurks a serious premise. Ultimately, however, *Young Frankenstein* is a movie about man's defiance of death.

This intellectual analysis was in marked contrast to the joyous insanity that appeared on the screen. Nationwide audiences flocked to see *Young Frankenstein.*

Journalist Herbert Gold said that when he saw the film in San Francisco, the audience began

screaming with laughter before the film went on
—a sure sign of cult in action.

The things that were funny to Mel Brooks were
the same things that were funny to Melvin Kaminsky on the corner of South Third and Hooper
forty years ago. They are funny to people all over
the country. "Tragedy," Brooks says, "is if I cut
my finger. Comedy is if I walk into an open
sewer." Humor is normal people in abnormal
situations, like Freddy Frankenstein returning to
Transylvania. Or it's abnormal people in ordinary
situations, like the monster, impeccably decked
out in evening clothes, tapping and singing "Puttin' on the Ritz." One critic said that the latter was
the funniest conception to appear in a comic film
since Chaplin's deadpan dinner of one roasted
shoe in *The Gold Rush*.

All kinds of people from all parts of the country flocked to see *Young Frankenstein*. The movie
was a particular hit with children who knew nothing of Mary Shelley's book, Lon Chaney or Bela
Lugosi, or *shtick* humor. Brooks had known since
*Get Smart* that kids were especially attracted to
his style. Noting the enthusiastic reception that the
seven-to-twelve set gave *Frankenstein* at sneak
previews, Brooks said, "I'll be the new Disney.
We're going to launch a whole new generation of
Mel Brooks freaks."

While Brooks was still subject to abuse from
the "crickets," he received an accolade that meant
more to him than one hundred rave reviews.
Director Frank Capra, speaking at the Institute of
Political Science at Harvard University in December 1975, criticized the new Hollywood with "its
arch cynicism and glittering decadence. Give me

something I can cheer about," said Capra. "Idealism is still what people care about." Capra had one kind word. "Hollywood would be lucky," said the master director, "if it had more Mel Brookses."

Interviewers noticed a new, more introspective Mel Brooks. Journalist Helen Dudar commented, "The end of the visit is Mel Brooks adorable: he leads you to the door pronouncing you a pussycat and planting energetic avuncular kisses on your cheek. But the beginning—the beginning is something else. Then, eyes wary, compact little body coiled against the protective arm of the couch, he asks questions. They are puzzling questions until you understand that he is determining whether you come as friend or foe. There you are, a charter fan who cackled through early Brooks epics in movie houses half-filled with otherwise morose audiences, a person who travels in a smart set composed exclusively of nuts who can recite entire Brooks records, and he can't tell at a glance; he wants to know, do you love me? Do you respect me?

"My goodness, YES."

Seemingly inexhaustible in earlier years, Brooks had tired of the high expectation of reporters and talk show hosts. He put interviewers on notice that he no longer did "a number." "I disappoint a lot of people that interview me," he said. "Because they have a preconception. You're always a little disappointing in person because you can't be the edited essence of yourself."

After the success of *Young Frankenstein*, Brooks was literally buried in print. During one interview, he impressed Helen Dudar as being "ferociously preoccupied with image. That is perhaps a natural consequence of having become the media person of the month," said Miss Dudar. "Twice in two hours, he mentions Jerry Lewis and what he feels is the distasteful press attention Lewis excited at the height of his fame ten years ago.

" 'People treated him like a chimp, not a person,' Brooks said with anger. 'It was terrible. They created a monster. And he was torn—he didn't want to let people down. They came to see Jerry Lewis, a jumping maniac. Who expected to see a father? A movie executive?' "

Indeed, Brooks had become more thoughtful, more concerned with his own character. Often too busy in the past to be reflective, he had come upon a new interest in life—discovering the real Mel Brooks.

He had always had a reputation for being an unusual interviewee. "Don't feel restricted," Brooks told *Post* columnist Jerry Tallmer during one interview, "but don't say what I say." "The problem is," said Tallmer, "to sort out when he's 'on,' doing his *shtick*, his thing, which is all the time, from when he's *off*, speaking as himself, which is some part of all that time 'even when he's on."

"There's never been a real me in a movie," he told Tallmer. "There's never been a real me on television, there isn't a real me right now in this interview. I keep thinking: Does that sound good? You always attempt to denigrate yourself in these things, and then to get loose and get back to the real you. I am not the 2000-Year-Old Man. I am not merely an *amusant*, a *divertissement*. I am a person even as they [his interviewers] are."

"It was several minutes later," commented

Tallmer, "that Brooks made his cat-screech, as he had once on the old Sid Caesar *Show of Shows*. . . . A waiter froze in his tracks; two men dining across the way revolved in their seats with as much cool as they could muster."

Perhaps the only interviewer who has not found Brooks likable was the luckless Joan Barthel, the *Life* magazine journalist who had been unfortunate enough to interview Brooks on the set of *The Producers*. Barthel has written about such luminaries as John Wayne, Henry Fonda, and Marian Anderson and is considered a first-rate biographical profile writer. Of her Brooks Waterloo she commented: "I'm sure I deserve the Purple Heart."

# 11

## The Cult

The reviews for *Young Frankenstein* were better than any Brooks had received before, indicating that the comedy writing team of Brooks and Wilder might try another screenplay. But despite their success, Brooks hesitated to collaborate with Gene Wilder on another script.

He was not and is not interested merely in success and good reviews. He is more interested in developing and expressing his own ideas, even if he fails. To this end he didn't want to direct a screenplay that he had not written himself. Wilder, already at work on another script, hoped that Brooks would reconsider and direct it for him. When he realized that Brooks didn't want to, he was forced to find another director. As an actor, Wilder saw himself almost as a *creation* of Mel Brooks. He said in a recent interview, "I'm his protégé, his child, and in some ways, his monster."

Brooks and Wilder are very different creative personalities. It seems possible that in *Young Frankenstein* there were artistic, if not personal, tensions. One visitor to the set saw Brooks banging his head against the wall shouting to Gene, "Only for you would I do this."

Brooks, however, did not put his protégé out in the cold without some protection. Mel determined long before that if Wilder was going to continue writing screenplays, he would have to learn to direct his own films. Throughout the shooting of *Young Frankenstein*, Brooks kept Wilder by his side, pointing out, step by step, the director's art.

Watching Brooks work was Wilder's first experience in film direction. Every day he sat by Brooks's side as he edited the film.

"Mel would say, 'Do you know the trouble I'm in because I didn't shoot that closeup? Don't do that.'

"I would say, 'To whom are you talking?'

" 'You, when you're directing.'

" 'Directing *what*?'

" 'Never mind,' he said. He became more and more intense, like a mother bird before shoving her baby off the limb."

When Brooks refused to direct Wilder's new script, he forced the actor-writer into the defensive position of director.

Wilder's reasons for heeding Brooks's command to direct were similar to Brooks's own. "I am not a comedian," Wilder said. "More than anything, I am an actor, I wanted to find parts I couldn't find. I don't want to write just to write. I want to write mainly to find a part that I want to act. And I want to direct in order to protect what I wrote, which I wrote in order to act."

Thus prepared, Wilder set upon his first directorial task. Wilder's new script was also a spoof, this time of the inimitable Sherlock Holmes. He decided that the central figure of the satire could not be Sherlock himself. "I don't think you can make fun of someone everyone reveres," he said.

In response, he created an insanely jealous younger brother, Sigerson Holmes ("S. Holmes, Consulting Investigator").

Wilder made his film in London, co-starring with other members of the traditional Brooks stock company: Madeline Kahn, Marty Feldman, and Dom DeLuise.

"I did not have as good a director as the other actors did," he said. "Their director was loving and patient. The director I had was sober, serious, and intolerant. He was bored watching me, and in general was a pain. I would have fired him, but he and the writer ganged up on me."

"He's been very gentle," said Madeline Kahn. "Taking people aside and having talks with them. He's almost inhumanly sweet. Sometimes I feel like a savage beside him."

"I am on a tightrope," Wilder says about his style. "I want an explosion of laughter on one side and Chopin on the other. Laughter is always the foot that gets me in the door," he told Mel Gussow of *The New York Times*, holding up his foot for emphasis. "But I want more than comedy."

*The Adventures of Sherlock Holmes' Smarter Brother* did well in previews. But the ultimate judgment, in Gene Wilder's eyes, was Mel Brooks's opinion. When Brooks screened the picture, he was at first silent. Then he laughed. Soon, said Wilder, he laughed louder than anyone. Asked what he would have done if Brooks hadn't liked the movie, Wilder replied morosely, "I would have been destroyed."

With the release of *Sherlock*, Wilder joined the slender ranks of comedy directors. Now he was subject to comparison with Brooks and Woody Allen. Wilder's debut was greeted with much the same tone of reservation that Brooks had encountered a few years earlier. Richard Schickel, however, writing for *Time* magazine, liked the film and considered Wilder's sensibilities even more childlike than those of Brooks.

Of his own style, Gene said, "I love definite things, I loved World War II films about Hitler, because you could say, 'Ah, the black moustache, that's evil.' I like pictures that are human, with people who are not perfect but who are definite in their characters."

Wilder acts comedy in opposites. When he was kidnapped in *Bonnie and Clyde*, he said, "I decided that the funniest thing was not to cower but to pretend that I was not afraid. Humor comes in how you hide, not how you show feeling."

Wilder attributes many of his comic insights to Mel Brooks. Since he has also been directed by Woody Allen (he was the man with a passion for sheep in *Everything You Always Wanted to Know about Sex*) he is in a position to compare these two giants of film comedy. "Woody Allen sets safety matches of topical jokes," said Wilder, "sometimes against classical themes—to counterpoint them—as in *Love and Death*. He sets maybe a thousand safety matches. They flare up, make you laugh, and die down. There is a physical humor in what he does, but the base is cerebral.

"Mel Brooks wants to set off atom blasts of humor. He is not interested in titters. He considers titters a failure. He is not interested in intellectual jokes. He wants gigantic explosions, so loud, so fierce that God and his father—Mel Brooks's father, they're both the same person—will hear. Mel is the Ritz Brothers, Olsen and Johnson, and the Marx Brothers. If you ever get serious on him, he'll lay banana peels in your path. His philosophical statement is laughter."

So few film comedies are being made today that reviewers tend to mention Woody Allen and Mel Brooks in the same breath, or try to pit the two against each other. But more and more, each had demanded and received individual acknowledgment for his virtues as well as his faults.

Allen is considered more intellectual than Brooks, a more concentrated writer. Statements that he has let drop over the last few years reveal that Brooks, too, would like to write more subtly —the sorts of things that appear under Allen's by-line in *The New Yorker*.

Brooks, however, is not competitive with Allen because he believes their styles and ideas are different. He is generous in his praise, calling Allen's work "poetic" and "perceptive." Brooks clearly admires his rival and does not hesitate to say so.

The two comics are ideally suited to appreciate the other's work—both the jokes and the more serious overtones of social and artistic commentary.

Melvin Kaminsky and Alan Stewart Konigsberg share a common background, Brooklyn, and a common outlook, which might be described as Jewish Wry. From a certain point of view—like over six feet tall—they are similar physically too. Both are small, unprepossessing men, though Allen plays it up as part of his public persona, and Brooks's physical energy makes him appear bigger than he is. Both men are intensely ambitious by any standards. The fact that they have managed to carve out successful careers as film directors, a business that few comedians have ever had the stamina to tackle, attests to the quality of their drive and endurance.

But where Allen is understated and apparently contemplative, Brooks is boisterous and seemingly thoughtless. While Brooks admires the sophisticated styles of Chaplin and Keaton, he owes less to these classical comedians than to the highly physical comedy of Laurel and Hardy and the Ritz Brothers.

As a comic, Mel Brooks rightly belongs in the ranks of George Burns, Milton Berle, Jack Benny, and the Marx Brothers, although he is many years their junior. Like these older comics, Brooks has the special outlook of a child of immigrants reared in the ghetto. It wasn't his grandparents or great-grandparents who came over on the ship, but his very own parents. As a child, Brooks thought he would grow up to speak Yiddish, too. English was a kid's language. When he grew up, he expected to speak Yiddish, just like his mother and the other grownups.

For these comics and for Mel Brooks a generation later, the early years were spent in a serenely Semitic world. It was only later they found out that the Jew is practically synonymous with "Outsider." By then it was too late. They had already developed a security, in fact an aggressiveness, in their own identities that would mark them the rest of their lives. It made their humor very different from the Jewish comedians who would follow them. Lenny Bruce, defensive and belligerent; Woody Allen, understated and slightly apologetic; David Steinberg, polished and perceptive—all would recognize and build upon their identities as outsiders enforced by society.

Brooks shows anger but not viciousness. Anger

at what? Anger, he says, "for being short. For not being born Franklin D. Roosevelt or Johnny Weissmuller—just a lot of hatred." But he didn't hate being Jewish.

The humor of Mel Brooks can be cruel and wild, but it is not black. His characters, from the *2000-Year-Old Man* to *Young Frankenstein*, are loving recreations of Jewish "types." They are not parodies or imitations. Brooks feels that Jewish humor, if not accurately and lovingly done, can be in bad taste. And he is a man who knows what bad taste is all about. He's been criticized for anal humor, crudeness, and craziness. But no one has yet accused him of anti-Semitism. It is this attitude that makes his Jewish humor so easy to take. He has managed to fuse the frantic Jewish nuttiness of Jerry Lewis with the iconoclasm of Lenny Bruce. And somehow, Brooks is without the bitterness that sometimes mars each of those two very different Jewish comics.

There are certain similarities between Brooks and Woody Allen. Both of the princes of modern comedy have a finely honed sense of language. It is surely no accident that, although years apart in age, both come from Jewish parentage, and both get comic mileage from the speech patterns of that milieu. Woody and Mel find hilarious any juxtaposition of the immigrant style with severely modern situations. Take, for example, Allen's routine about the men from outer space who force all earthlings to go into the tailoring business in order to supply the aliens with pants. Or look at the *2000-Year-Old Man*. The only joke in that whole routine is the comparison of a typical Yiddish grandpa with images of the giants of ancient history.

Brooks's material relates to his Jewishness and the experience of growing up Jewish. He credits his mother as the source of his comedic style. "My mother had this exuberant joy of living," he said, "and she infected me with that. She really was responsible for the growth of my imagination. She told us stories when we were unhappy, crying, and bitter, she always managed to somehow jolly us out of it."

The accent Brooks uses for some of his characters is what he calls an American-Jewish accent. He thinks it will disappear in fifty years and its passing will be a great loss.

Brooks described to journalist Larry Wilde how his mother's speech pattern and inflections influenced such characters as the 2000-Year-Old Man. "My mother had a way of bombastically attacking when she was happy. She'd say, 'What're you talkin'?' It's very difficult to explain. I remember she told me that when I was a baby somebody would say to her, 'Oh, what a beautiful baby you have!' And she'd say, 'What're you talkin', *beautiful*? He's *gorgeous*!' . . . Almost with anger."

Given the similarities of their background, the two rivals for top spot in the world of movie comedy approach their subject from opposite angles. Brooks is a street comedian. His humor is first of all physical—running, leaping, grimacing —all the activities that accompany any corner boy's stories. Allen, on the other hand, is a loner. His humor develops first in his head. Then, it is verbal, and the physical and visual qualities follow.

Woody Allen and Mel Brooks have both created "repertory companies"—groups of people who work mainly with either one or the other. Both command a great deal of loyalty from those who work with them, personal as well as professional.

It is rare in the world of moviemaking, where paranoia is the general rule, for directors to work with their friends. Usually a friendship with a director or producer of the stature of Woody Allen or Mel Brooks means that you will never be hired for the friend's films. But Allen and Brooks seem to develop symbiotic relationships that go beyond the status of either professional or social.

But while Brooks's cohorts such as Gene Wilder and Madeline Kahn have developed important careers outside the nest, Allen regulars like Tony Roberts and Diane Keaton seem to do little without their mentor. One reason may be a difference in style. The focus of a film written and directed by Woody Allen is usually the performer and the *character*—Woody Allen. While Roberts, or Keaton, or Allen's ex-wife Louise Lasser, may turn in superlative performances, it is always Allen himself who is the center of the camera's attention. Brooks, much as he loves to perform, is always a secondary character (or two) in his own films. In fact, Brooks had cast himself as the unregenerate Nazi in *The Producers* until he saw Kenneth Mars audition. Mars auditioned well and Brooks gave him the part.

The most common remark about both Woody Allen and Mel Brooks is that they are both at home with the language, and use it always to their comic advantage. Of the two, Allen is considered to have a greater intellectual linguistic command. His work seems to be more polished than Brooks's. But there is a territory—the land of the belly laugh and pure physical action—where Brooks reigns supreme. "His humor," says Peter Boyle, "is a punch and a jab. It's visceral."

Others, like Gene Wilder, recognize a new maturity in Brooks. "Mel is in transition from a maker of wonderful films to a film director," says Wilder. "He used to just want to set up the camera and let the characters and situation rule—afraid that if there wasn't a laugh on every count of ten he was letting the audience down. Now, he says, 'Let's not chase two rabbits. We've got time.'"

Wilder believes that Brooks's humor does have a philosophical base, and is getting deeper all the time. Wilder believes that Brooks is after lasting comedy, immortality in fact. Brooks speaks, in Wilder's view, to the basics of the human condition—greed, frustration, conflicting desires. These are the elements of the human personality that will be around as strongly two hundred years from now as they are today.

Along with this new maturity goes a yearning to do something more serious and understated. In some ways, Brooks believes he should have continued as a writer and ignored directing. Directing and production take a great deal of time. Brooks is a man who has many things to say.

Given complete artistic freedom, what kind of picture would Brooks make? He'd like to do a "bittersweet comedy" about death; something he fears the critics and the public would roast him for right now. But he would do this in some little off-off Broadway theater where no one's money would get hurt.

His major artistic goals are not and never have been political. And while Mel was on the fringes of the show business left-wingers in the early Fifties, he has made no identifiable public political statement in many years.

Of course he could not be a Republican. Some Jews have tried it and their very genes have rebelled against such heresy. Mel is too much a Jew to be a Republican. But American Jews have always been intensely political, and Brooks has given few indications of his personal politics. It is entirely possible that he casts a write-in vote for F.D.R. whenever he gets the chance and lets it go at that.

The very thrust of his work is antipolitical. Mel is always bursting balloons, pricking pomposity, wrestling righteousness. He is, it seems, against all politicians, the forerunner of a truly happy anarchistic Jewish society.

Or maybe he thinks his politics are his own business.

Recently, Brooks allied himself with the Hollywood political left to make a statement about the rights of the filmmakers.

Hollywood was severely jolted when movie figures were linked with the notorious Weather Underground. Prominent documentary filmmaker Emile de Antonio, film editor Mary Lampson, and Academy-Award-winning cameraman-director Haskell Wexler were subpoenaed to appear before a Los Angeles grand jury, along with film and tape pertaining to a documentary they were filming on the Weather Underground. Indictments were reported to be imminent against various unnamed actors and actresses for allegedly giving financial aid to the fugitives. The three filmmakers argued that the subpoenas raised substantial questions of governmental censorship.

Brooks came forward with several dozen of Hollywood's best known names including Hal Ashby, Warren Beatty, Peter Bogdanovich, Jeff Bridges, Peter Fonda, Shirley MacLaine, Jack Nicholson, Arthur Penn, Rip Torn, Jon Voight, and Robert Wise, in support of "the right of these people to make a film about any subject, and specifically the right of these people to make a film about the Weather Underground." The subpoenas were shortly withdrawn.

Brooks relates better to sex and food, he says, than to politics. "I love spaghetti and sex, sometimes together. My dream of heaven is walking naked through fields of pasta fazool."

But, for the most part, both Allen and Brooks resist intellectual labels. They are above all interested in the mass appeal of their comedy. Yet they seek the fundamental themes—isolation, boredom, loss of love—and give these a comic twist that is unique in the history of modern humor.

Brooks says he is not concerned about whether he or Woody Allen is the true king of the funny bone. Box-office figures show that *Blazing Saddles* out-grossed *Sleeper*, which gives the title, in a technical sense at least, to Brooks. But, as Mel has said, "Woody and I don't get in each other's way." Far from stealing each other's audiences, the appetite for one is fed by consumption of the other. If someone goes to a Mel Brooks movie and loves it, he is more likely to pick another comedy for his next cinematic outing.

While indebted to the insanely physical school of film comedies, Brooks also is enamored of the later, more subtle comedy films of Ernst Lubitsch and Billy Wilder, who made what Brooks calls the "shining" comedies of the Thirties. Although it is not his style to imitate these controlled, elaborately conceived films, he admires them. He is disappointed that the single recent attempt to do a comic film in the Lubitsch style—Peter Bogdanovich's *At Long Last Love*—was unsuccessful. The critics again failed to see the film for what it was, missing the subtleties and perfection of style.

Occasionally, Brooks will try to verbalize the essence of comedy. "Comedy," he says, "is not surprise, it's knowing. How does it work, how does it laminate? Seeing it on the horizon, expecting, unable to stop it."

But for the most part he leaves theorizing to critics. All the observation in the world won't make a comic. Brooks trusts his instincts. He makes no apologies for the jokes that misfire. Mel figures that his slapdash approach to laughs reassures, perhaps even flatters, the audience: "Look, he got away with that bad joke? Why can't I?"

Brooks is an old-time movie fan. He appreciates many kinds of films, and criticizes his "crickets" for not liking films as much as they should. Brooks does not demand that films meet his own personal frame of reference. He extends himself to try to enjoy a movie for what it has to offer. He can enjoy what he calls a popcorn movie such as *Dr. Zhivago* just as much as he does the Ritz Brothers. He appreciates a film for what it is. Of *Dr. Zhivago*, he says: "You mustn't listen to the dialogue too carefully, you mustn't examine the relationships, you mustn't try to see Omar Sharif as a Russian."

Brooks admires David Lean, director of *Dr. Zhivago* and *Lawrence of Arabia*. Lean has as clearly recognizable a style as Brooks, even though they differ totally. But Brooks likes to poke fun at Lean's giant-sized movies. "Think of David Lean making a dirty movie," he says. "First of all, it has to be the biggest room in the world, right? Because he has to move the camera back a thousand yards. Then he wants heat shimmer, so it has to be shot in the Sahara Desert."

Brooks's own early films were usually low budget profit-makers. *The Producers*, budgeted at under $1 million, cleared a neat $5 million in its first year.

In general, Brooks is reluctant to say anything bad about any of his colleagues in the movie industry. Did he like *Love Story*, then, if he's such a movie buff? Does he appreciate that kind of audience manipulation that has whole theaters full of people crying their eyes out?

"You know, I got exactly the same reaction in the cutting room of *The Producers*. There they were, Joe Levine and everybody, all sobbing and weeping and saying: "What have we got here? We're gonna lose money."

As Brooks says, comedy is a dangerous business. When a comedy film fails, the word gets around very quickly. As with a standup comic, the comedy film suffers only two responses: terrific or terrible. The film industry is especially conservative about giving money to madmen, unless the madmen, like Brooks, make money.

The successes racked up by *Sleeper* and *Blazing Saddles* were a signal for the money men to start pouring money into all-out laughter. Even so, no one today besides Brooks and Allen and now Gene Wilder, is trusted enough by financial backers to be given a free directorial hand. Wilder and Brooks each have signed a three-picture deal with Twentieth Century-Fox to write and direct three more films. Wilder's next is *When the Right Man Comes Along*, a comedy mystery. And Brooks's latest is *Silent Movie*.

It's been reported that Brooks personally would make $5 million from *Young Frankenstein*. He is indignant. "People don't understand the finances of movies," he complained. "They don't even know what 25 percent of the gross for distributing means. I'll be very lucky to make $100,000 or $200,000—and that would be a bloody fortune.

"You know when that happens? This $5 million? It happens with a *Godfather*, a *Sting*, when a picture makes $100 million.

"I got calls from relatives all over the world. It's very embarrassing. I feel like a failure, you know what I mean?

"Anyway, I don't make movies for money. I never did. Of course you want a lot of people to see them. But I never expected *Blazing Saddles* to make a quarter. It was a very private joke that the world joined me in. Who knew they knew? But obviously—they knew."

If Brooks himself is not realizing millions from his pictures, the studio is. And so they are willing to finance just about any film he wants to make. Brooks has a vision of success on his own terms. "If you work at a lower level," he says, "you burn out, you become flashpaper." As his stature grows, his artistic freedom expands.

When he speaks of television and movies, Brooks compares the artistic values of the media with such artists as Samuel Beckett, James Joyce, and Pablo Picasso. Regardless of the form, the material has to "breathe right." The goal of his future work is to get down to the essence of feeling. "And yet as a writer," he says, "I know that without a story there's no tension. So that's the problem I'm trying to synthesize . . . how to get by with the least amount of a story."

But in the same breath, Brooks scoffs at the pretentions of art and artists. "My job is you should pay three dollars and not want to spit at the ticket-taker on the way out."

Money, then, like so many other parts of Brooks's life, plays a paradoxical role. Primarily, he makes films to express his own ideas, and if the public likes them that's terrific. Secondly, he makes films to reach people. Finally, he hopes the films turn a profit. He clearly outlines these steps. But on the other hand, the importance of the steps must be reversed if Brooks is going to continue as a filmmaker. His films must make money; for them to make money they must command a wide audience; and if they make money and command a wide audience, then Brooks has enough freedom to express his ideas and make any kind of film he wishes. Therefore, does Mel Brooks make movies to make money? Maybe he does and maybe he doesn't. His main slogan these days is "Funny is money."

Brooks was fortunate in having the Caesar show as a training ground. Caesar's writers were allowed freedom of their own judgment. He learned to trust his instincts, and he learned that what he thought was funny was closely aligned with what other people thought was funny. Today Brooks's style and the expectations of the public are similar. But Brooks himself created the desire for people to see his kind of comedy, and then filled the need. Therefore it's difficult to separate money from Brooks's goals.

Brooks is a peculiar blend of *avant garde* and commercial. Although he talks of doing little experimental plays off Broadway, he would probably instinctively make the play into a hit. His comedy is original and unconventional, yet it is easily appreciated by the public at large. While he believes he writes just for a choice few, his work appeals to millions. There is apparently a little Mel Brooks in us all.

Clearly Brooks does not have to worry whether he is sacrificing his artistic goals for the sake of a buck. He does not have to make the choices between commercial success and the kind of work he *really* wants to do. The two things are the same.

For the most part, everything he wants to do in the future has a commercially sound basis. Should he choose to do that special little experiment, then, as he says, he would do it so it wouldn't cost anything. He might, for example, want to do something serious. "I'm thinking of this good natured guy named Death, straw boater, good looking guy—*Excuse me, madam.* He picks up a girl, takes her in the alley, she comes out a withered ninety-seven-year-old crone. That kind of thing."

If he had to make a choice between successful commercial filmmaking and "art," Brooks would probably prefer making money. A commercially successful film pays the rent and guarantees that he will work again. Perhaps more important, more people see a successful film. Brooks loves the idea that his work has mass appeal. Better to have a blockbuster commercial hit than a classic "art" film that is shown occasionally at special film festivals.

But what about the artist's right to fail? In *The*

*Producers,* Brooks gave Max Bialystock a line in which he said, "I've struck a reef, I'm going. I'm a failure in a society that demands success. All I can deliver is failure." Though the movie is all about failure, Brooks doesn't see any right to fail in our society. He sees it as a myth, a mirage. He thinks it's a nice idea, but "there's no reason to it; there's no truth in it." He knows, however, that he may fail at any time. Does it frighten him? Perhaps. A little failure is acceptable. But he knows he had better be ready to back it up with a lot of success.

Brooks was on a clear winning streak with *Blazing Saddles* followed by *Young Frankenstein.* What happens when a long-shot winner stumbles on the track?

# 12

## When Things Were Rotten

A new atmosphere shadowed the television industry in 1975. Programming was being selected on a different basis than in the previous two or three years, when cops and robbers ruled the channels. Success of shows such as *All in the Family* and *Sanford and Son* had created a fresh demand for comedy. These shows and many other comedy programs of the 1970s owe a debt to *Get Smart* for initially breaking the mold of the standard situation comedy.

Other factors were also at work. Networks had agreed to adopt a designated "family viewing hour" between eight and nine o'clock every evening. They were forced to find alternatives to police adventure shows that would involve action without excessive violence. There was the further pressure of an uncertain economy. Networks didn't want to take any chances with the fall season's new programs. They wanted nothing short of guaranteed success. Who better to fill the bill than Melvin?

Brooks's involvement in a new television series came about when two writers, John Boni and Norman Stiles, called producer Norman Steinberg and suggested a satirical version of the Robin Hood legend. Steinberg took the idea to Brooks, with whom he had worked on *Blazing Saddles*. Without Brooks's participation, it is unlikely that any network would have been interested in the program. But with the new *wunderkind's* reputation as insurance, ABC agreed to pick up the hundred-thousand-dollar-per-episode tab.

After several years away from a weekly series, Brooks was as enthusiastic as ever about television. He felt a debt of gratitude to the medium. "After all," he said, "TV paid my bills for a long time." But he did not make a total commitment to the show, limiting his participation to consulting with the show's writers and producer.

The new program was called *When Things Were Rotten*. According to Brooks, since in the old days there were no dry cleaners or laundromats, when Robin Hood and his Merry Men rode on the bus they smelled rotten. Actually they were rancid, but, Brooks said, "rotten fits better into the title."

The technique of the Robin Hood show was similar to that of *Blazing Saddles*, the simultaneous juxtaposition of different periods of time by using contemporary dialogue and events in a period setting. In the bow and arrow contests, for example, there is Lord McDonald of the Golden Archers, with "Over 1 Million Dispatched" emblazoned on the back of his T-shirt. In the middle of a sedate court entertainment, a conga player appears to give a superb impersonation of Miguelito Valdez singing "Babalu." At the county fair, a sign reads, "Horse Parking . . . We Validate." And a white-haired gentleman with a goatee suddenly appears pushing a cart with the message, "Kensington Fried Pheasant . . . It's Knuckle-Lickin' Good."

"Silly is what we're after," Brooks said of the new show. "Nothing too sharp. Horsing around. When the Sheriff of Nottingham's tax collector tells the peasants to "hold their tongues," they literally stick out their tongues and grab them with their own hands."

The precise interpretation of commands was reminiscent of the old George Burns and Gracie Allen sketches, when Gracie comprehends only the exact literal meaning of words.

GEORGE BURNS: Say goodnight, Gracie.
GRACIE: Goodnight, Gracie.

Thus when one peasant refuses to hold his tongue, the tax collector says to the henchman, "Put him in his place!" And the four Mafiosi pound him over the head with sledge hammers and drive him into the ground until only his head is showing. "He's in his place, sir!"

The series was produced by Norman Steinberg, an ex-New York lawyer turned comedy writer. Steinberg described some of the characters in the show:

"Robin [played by Dick Gautier] is a real C.P.L.—Certified Public Legend—and his laughs come from his legendary behavior." Added Brooks: "We have the classic hero here who, by the way, we find out robs the rich but doesn't give everything to the poor. He keeps some money to run his administration."

Alan-A-Dale [Bernie Kopell] is a "medieval Las Vegas comic—he's the Greek chorus, the team historian-publicist who suddenly turns to the audience to enthuse, 'Now isn't that wonderful—isn't he brave and handsome?'

"Friar Tuck [Dick Van Patten] is the finest swordsman in all of England—with a knife and fork. A man of cloth and violence." Friar Tuck is determined never to let religion interfere with his gluttony. In one palace duel, the Friar, a sword in his right hand, munches a chicken in his left. When attacked from the left, he skewers the attacker with a chicken bone, then turns his head and bites into the sword.

The Sheriff of Nottingham [Henry Polic II] was "Primeval—presently separated from his wife." When the sheriff visits the dungeons the prisoners are moaning and weeping. It's music to his ears. "I must come down here more often," he says. "It's the only place I can really unwind."

Prince John, according to Brooks, "is a big swish. Giggles, wears earrings. Loves to gavotte. . . ."

Maid Marian [Misty Rowe] was a spy in the house of Prince John. She wanted to marry Robin right away and set up house in the model home going up in Rancho Sherwood Estates.

Richard Dimitri played dual roles, Bertram the Bad, and Renaldo, one of the Merry Men—identical twins separated at birth. As Bertram, Dimitri gave a devastating imitation of Laurence Olivier as *Richard III*. "Bertram," said Steinberg, "is really a cross between Sir Laurence Olivier and Charlie Chan's number one son. His twin, Renaldo, is 'Hispanic.' "

ABC bought the new series on the basis of the pilot—reported to be the funniest since *Get Smart*. While there were high expectations for the series at the network, it was tempered by questions of how long a burlesque of a single tale could be sustained and how much time Brooks himself would devote to the project.

The opening show had an abundance of sight gags, including signs such as "NOTTINGHAM NEXT THREE EXITS." In the medieval treasury, signs are posted: POSITIVELY NO PERSONAL CHECKS CASHED" and "FOREIGN EXCHANGE: ONE OF OURS FOR TWO OF THEIRS." The billboard leading to Sherwood reads: "WELCOME—NO POACHING, SCRAMBLING, FRYING OR HARD-BOILING."

Gaspard the Spy, who eavesdrops on Robin Hood in the forest, is disguised as a fruit tree. One day it's an apple tree, one day it's mixed fruit. When Gaspard goes to the Sheriff of Nottingham to get paid for his information, that day wearing his mixed-fruit ensemble, the sheriff picks grapes off of it, eats them, and tells his aide to pay him. "From the spy fund or the forestry fund?" queries the aide.

Down in the dungeons, where dissidents are being grilled and stretched, the sheriff and Prince John enter and order the victims to liven up. The chained prisoners instantly render a chorus of "Forget your troubles, come on get happy." One segment sees Bertram led blindfolded to Robin's forest hideaway—on a blindfolded horse. And when the tax collector is thrown through the air into a door, he is asked what took him so long to arrive. "Head winds," he said.

The pilot episode of *When Things Were Rotten* received generally good notices from the press. *Time* magazine felt that even if the show wasn't up to *Young Frankenstein* or even *Get Smart*, "it proved that second rate Brooks can come close to being first rate television." But most reviewers felt the situation was too limiting to provide situations for more than a few weeks. They also concurred that the success or failure of the show would depend on whether or not Mel Brooks wrote it himself.

Other weekly sagas included the appearance of a Dr. Strangelovian character hired by the sheriff to eradicate Robin, who brings with him the Ultimate Weapon—all the viewer sees is a twelve-foot trigger. In another episode, Robin and his Merry Men share quarters with the sheriff and his crowd—all quarantined with bubonic plague. Then Robin saves Maid Marian from the clutches of a wife-shopping sheik from a Middle Eastern fig-and-olive-picking country and, while Robin and the lads are vacationing on the ocean, the sheriff recruits a band of look-alikes to discredit him.

The concept of each show was a series of skits strung together, each with similar jokes. Unlike a variety show, however, the show was stuck with Robin Hood for a theme. Because there was little meaningful characterization, it became the same skit done over and over again. After a while, the adventures of Robin Hood just were not interesting any more.

Benjamin Stein of the *Wall Street Journal* was harsh in his appraisal of the new show. "Robin Hood is such a clean-cut though vain namby pamby he has no connection with the real world. The Sheriff of Nottingham is all bad, and he, too, is no one we know. The same is true for all the other characters. There are a few swishy looking types and having swishy characters in a medieval setting is supposed to be funny, but why is it? Brooks has confused the anomalous with the funny. In another scene, he puts a Cuban rhythm band at a castle party. It's bizarre, but not funny. Even the generous use of the laugh track doesn't make it funny."

Critics condemned the show for weak plot and poor writing. The directorial hand of Brooks clearly was missing from the show. The acting was self-conscious and "too cute by far," something that Brooks would never have permitted any of his stock company to do. The jokes were an aimless string of one-liners rather than part of a situation which in itself was comic.

Most of the criticism fell directly on Brooks's head. There was irony in some of the accusations. When Brooks made *The Producers*, many reviewers criticized him for being "too television oriented." He made movies, they said, as if he was writing sketches for television. Now with the release of *When Things Were Rotten*, the creator of *Your Show of Shows* and *Get Smart* was criticized for being a filmmaker. Benjamin Stein, who had worked himself into a rage over the Robin Hood show, rashly commented: "Brooks, for all his success in the movies, does not know how to make a television comedy take off."

Aside from Stein's peculiar evaluation of Brooks's television experience, the critics in this instance were proved correct in their analysis. There were several reasons why *When Things Were Rotten* was not a success. It was basically a one-joke situation. Unlike *Get Smart*, the new series did not have even an antihero for audiences to identify with. The constant use of misplaced time and context became irritating after a while. When an ancient bell is stolen from the tower, someone asks "What does it look like?"

"Oh, just one of those bells . . . that now and then rings," is the reply. And as Robin Hood rides off to fight the foe, a follower yells: "Buckle up for safety!" The gags now were expected, tedious, and unrelated to characters or story lines.

How much of this was Brooks's fault is hard to say. Certainly he is a writer who thinks first of character and motivation, secondly about gag lines. It may not seem so when you are watching a Brooks film, but the reason interest is maintained is because the jokes are logical and directly related to the character on the screen. *When Things Were Rotten* did not have this kind of thought behind it.

How did the failure of the television show affect Brooks's career? The worst he can be accused of, since he did not actually write the shows himself, is a lack of judgment. But judgment is what makes or breaks television producers. Norman Lear, for instance, must maintain a record number of successes in order to continue producing. It is doubtful, then, that Brooks will be involved in another series in the near future.

# 13

# The Heavyweight Champion of Comedy

For thirty years Brooks has been a cult hero. For most of that time, by any reasonable standards, he's been a financial and critical success. Since the achievement of *Your Show of Shows*, Brooks's place has been at the center of the inner circle, the holy of holies. At first he was a comic's comic and a comedy writer whose work was most appreciated by other comedy writers. He was the Master, the King, but only to those in the know. He chafed under the obscurity. Then came *Blazing Saddles*. It changed his life, not the inner Brooks, but the outer circumstances. Before, he was most appreciated by close friends at parties. Today, he spends most of his time being the King of the Realm—everybody's realm.

There is no one more "arrived" than Mel Brooks. And he intends to stay there. Although he murmurs that he feels he has earned the right to fail, to make films that interest him regardless of their box-office appeal, his primary goal is still to be the funniest. Funny is money, as he says, but funny is also a life goal. His close friend, novelist Joseph Heller, claims that no one will ever again see Brooks at his funniest, a level achieved in olden days when he could be heard hilariously savaging colleagues who had made it. But now Brooks has made it. With his success has come a new mellowness and circumspection. His vicious, devilish side is more hidden. People love Mel Brooks. And Brooks is shrewd enough to know that lovability is one of his main assets. Any hostility he feels is obliterated by the sheer lovability of his personality.

Brooks is genuinely adorable, although he also knows how to make people love him. During the taping of *The David Susskind Show*, Brooks monopolized the conversation of a group which included David Steinberg, writer Dan Greenberg, and fashion designer Mr. Mort. While Brooks blasted out anything that came into his head, Steinberg—who has a deadly accurate sophisticated wit—sat thinking, all wheels turning. Whenever Mel would take a breath, Steinberg would shoot out his prepared line. Obviously admiring each other, the two comedians stole the show.

Dan Greenberg, on the other hand, seemed irritated to be left out. In the presence of such high powered performing talent, the writer appeared sullen. When Susskind asked his opinion, Greenberg replied sulkily, "Why ask me?" Obviously piqued because he was not the center of attention, Greenberg deliberately withdrew from the conversation; if he had to compete he wasn't interested. Brooks, going his rollicking haphazard way, seemed not to notice. But who else, as the program neared an end, could have turned the charm on Greenberg? No one but lovable Mel. With the utmost sensitivity Brooks directed questions at Greenberg, listened to the answers, and before one's eyes, Greenberg became alive again; he could not resist Melvin at his best.

Melvin is a big director now, one of the few who is allowed to make any kind of film he chooses. His most recent work is a silent film. It is called *Mel Brooks's Silent Movie*. Unlike the original silents, Brooks's film was done in color, but it has written titles rather than dialogue. Brooks's idea is that comic scenes should explain themselves visually.

Silent movies, much more than talkies, need to capture the audience's full attention to succeed. If the movie is good, if the image tells the story, the audience can't take its eyes away from the screen. It is a much more involving medium. There should be no need for dialogue; and only a small need for titles. Besides color, the one concession to modern technology in Brooks's film is sound effects.

Brooks has become a film purist. He believes, along with other serious filmmakers, that movies are foremost a visual medium. "When something talks too much," he says, "it's a play. When something moves a lot, it's a film." He has no patience with movies that are conversations between two people. He likes chase scenes, lots of movement: running, falling, bopping, sliding wildly into each other with arms flailing. He conceives his ideas in terms of film without dialogue. The visual image is primary, the connective idea secondary, in much the same way that a painter visualizes his canvas first, then discovers the idea behind the image.

The new silent movie is about a company called Engulf and Devour—you can take your pick of which multinational conglomerate it represents

—which takes over a small, sweet movie studio called Sunshine Studios. Sunshine, says Brooks, is in the business of providing art, happiness, and joy. E & D wants to tear Sunshine down and put up a shopping center. The studio chief, who, naturally, wears feathers, calls on Mel Funn, genius director, to save the studio by coming up with a blockbuster movie idea. Funn, who has been absent from the scene for a few years because of a drinking problem, gives every appearance of not having sobered up yet. Mel Funn, of course, is played by Melvin.

Brooks gathered together some of his rotating stock company to assume other starring roles: Dom DeLuise and Marty Feldman were, as usual, present and eager to go. Funn decides that the only thing to save Sunshine would be, yes, a silent movie. The chief, hearing the plan, faints dead away. "Why go backwards?" the studio chief cries to Mel Funn. Funn answers, "Because there's more fun in backwards than forwards—or even than now."

*Mel Brooks's Silent Movie* whips in and out of reality just as *Blazing Saddles* did. In the end of *Saddles*, the entire cast, engaged in a classic western brawl, breaks through the wall of an adjoining soundstage where a campy musical—tails and top hats—is being shot. Cleavon Little ducks out to Grauman's Chinese Theater and watches—you guessed it—*Blazing Saddles*.

In the same way, it is difficult to separate the story line of *Silent Movie* from the reality of Brooks's life.

Like Mel Funn, Mel Brooks is reckoned with in Hollywood these days as a kind of natural phenomenon—a tidal wave or a typhoon. Every-

one from novelist to neophyte is curious about
Brooks and fascinated by whatever details they
find. Interviews abound. What does he look like,
really? What does he wear? What does he eat,
besides Raisinettes? What is Brooks's philosophy
or theory or whatever it is that enables him to keep
piling up one hit after another? People hunger for
details about this latest manifestation of pure
laughter, and Brooks, ever the extrovert, is not
stingy with quotable quotes.

Physically, Brooks is mainly short, and he's no
longer the skinny kid he used to be, though by no
means fat. He turned fifty on June 28, 1976, but
he looks like a little boy. Basketball motions
come naturally to him as he describes a comedian
"who just holds the ball till it's green and moldy."
"What do I like?" he inquires. "Sex and spaghetti,
spaghetti and sex." He asks naive, intimate questions in a childlike way. He talks about his
mother, with whom he burns up the telephone
wires weekly between Hollywood and Miami, and
shows visitors the transparent plastic cube with
the pictures of his children.

Like many comics, Brooks has an incredibly
mobile face which he keeps in motion, thus
making it hard to describe his features. In repose
—a rare moment—his face is appealing, masculine, lovable, even handsome. Brooks, of course,
makes the most of his rubber face. Handsomeness
doesn't pay off for a comic, with the glorious exception of Cary Grant. He is most often photo-
graphed gesturing, mugging, or posing in some
outlandish costume. His dress is subject to varia-
tion. He may be dressed up in a feather bonnet
or chasing a bosomy blonde in his shorts, T-shirt,
and garters, eyes-crossed, as in *Blazing Saddles*.

Occasionally, when he's dressed up in a dark suit and tie, he looks like an adman. Most often, he wears his directing outfit, slacks and an open shirt topped with a pullover.

He has a flock of awards—gold records, two Academy awards, an Emmy, and special Writers' Guild gold plaques—"and they all live together in harmony and happiness on my mother's television set in Miami Beach."

The things that hurt him in the old days have lost some of their sting now that he can talk to reporters across a mammoth desk in his own office located in the dream world of the Twentieth Century-Fox back lot. The size of his office, falling only somewhat short of a basketball court, testifies to the fact that he's made it. His conversation no longer has the frantic pace of a standup routine. Brooks knows how offensive success can be to other people. He has seen others die from the syndrome, and he learned his lessons well. Success will not kill Mel Brooks. He controls it, never letting his ego run away with him. He shows off his success and denigrates it at the same time.

His interviews now are notably more relaxed and serious. Is Brooks an ambitious man? He gives the reporter a cross-eyed look. Is Rubinstein a piano player? Of course he's ambitious. In a field as competitive as show business, not to have overwhelming ambition is suicide for a career. But Mel Brooks exceeds even the normally high level of striving that characterizes his profession. He needs to win, needs it badly. He's willing to swing out of windows for it, risk his very own neck for it.

One part of winning that a comedian is nearly always denied is serious critical recognition.

Chaplin has it, but Chaplin is so old now that even critics are sentimental over him. When he was in his prime, producing films that now make audiences around the world weep with laughter, Chaplin was often a target for public and critical abuse.

Keaton and Lloyd have it, but Keaton and Lloyd are dead. The great Groucho has lived long enough to see himself honored by serious people, and he revels in it. But what about the people who are working today, turning out what must surely be tomorrow's comedy classics? For them, for all comedy writers everywhere, there is very little intellectual recognition. It hurts Mel Brooks that this is so, just as it hurts Woody Allen and it hurt Lenny Bruce. But it may be inevitable, because people believe—even when they say they don't—that funny things are inconsequential things.

But ask him if he thinks his own work will survive a half-century and he turns salty. Recent reviewers have elevated him to the status of "a serious artist," a heavy label he refuses to admit he enjoys. "I'm sure when Chaim Soutine finished *The Bellboy* he did not take ten steps away and say, 'That is a great work of art.' Maybe he hoped somebody might say it a hundred years later. But what he probably said was, 'I'm so glad I finished it.' "

He may feel that certain comic artists are greater than those artists who take the world seriously. But he knows that no matter what he thinks, a comic will never receive the same prestige as a serious artist.

So Brooks concentrates on his work. "Immortality is a by-product of good work. Masterpieces are not for artists, they're for critics. Critics can't even make music by rubbing their back legs together. My message to the world is 'Let's swing, sing, shout, make noise! Let's be wet and noisy!' "

How does the self-confident Brooklyn boy feel when his work is compared in the press to that of Bellow, Malamud, Arthur Miller, and others of that elite group of Jewish novelists—all of them very serious artists—who have brought the subject of Jewish individualism to the attention of the public? He's flattered but not astounded. He respects all of those writers, but reserves his heaviest admiration for his friend, Joe Heller, author of *Catch 22* and *Something Happened.* Heller, like Brooks, is unpretentious. Brooks, in fact, could be called aggressively unpretentious. Years ago a friend also said of Anne Bancroft that she was "pretentiously unpretentious." Unpretentiousness seems to be a life goal with Brooks and Bancroft. The down-home quality they each profess is one of choice, rather than affectation. Brooks is a man always aware of his image . . . but the image changes from moment to moment. He is erudite or he is aggressively illiterate. His language alternates between street-jargon Jewish and intellectual literary. But there are still basic fundamentals that are consistent in his character. He respects work and people who are dedicated to their work. And he enjoys the real world of nonartistic consideration, such as Chinese food and spaghetti.

The things Mel Brooks loves are resolutely of the here and now: friendship, love, his children, money, sex, spaghetti, Raisinettes, art, books, and above all Anne Bancroft. He despises one thing, death, and he freely admits it. But he doesn't believe that immortality comes from straining solemnly after masterpieces. What defeats death is life, lived with as much juice as you can somehow induce to flow.

One of the main elements of his character is a touching personal loyalty which borders on possessiveness. It's a quality which all his friends emphasize when discussing him. "Good things happen to people who know Mel," says one of his producers. But he relieves his chronic anxiety by controlling the world around him and taking charge of every situation he finds himself in. "He's a typical Jewish mother," says a friend. "He orders your lunch for you, tells you what kind of car you should buy, suggests good doctors and nice operations you could have." "But Mel's advice is always good," adds another of his friends. "He's the sanest maniac I've ever met."

He has made a family for himself where he is both child and father. Herbert Gold wrote of Brooks, "His metabolism is driven by a heart which defies the loss of his father, the loss of childhood, by insisting that childhood is everywhere."

People have noticed that in his movies, boy rarely gets girl, even though most of his movies have happy endings. In his first three movies, in fact, boy gets boy. Zero Mostel gets Gene Wilder, Frank Langella gets Ron Moody, Gene Wilder gets Cleavon Little. It may be coincidence, but there may be a deeper significance. Brooks admits that the reason goes all the way back to his childhood. He credits his need to have his male characters come together and be close, to a displaced association with his father, whom he really never knew. The loss of his father is still a source of pain to him. When Brooks has male characters in his movies find each other, he expresses his long-ing to find his father and be close to him. Many men, even those who grew up with both parents, often feel deprived of an expression of love from their father. It is interesting that men who watch these Brooks scenes are almost always moved by the recreation of a close father and son relation-ship.

Is Brooks—one of the most valued and re-spected directors in the business—any different from the kid who moved props in Red Bank, New Jersey, nearly thirty years ago? Will Jordan doesn't think so. Jordan recently visited Brooks on the set of *Silent Movie*. "I hadn't seen him in several years," Jordan said. "He was just the same. Warm, interested, marvelous to talk to. He has total recall, you know. He remembered details from those days that I had forgotten. He's just the sweetest guy in the world."

Success has not spoiled Brooks. If anything, it's made him more easy-going and sympathetic. "I used to be very hard to live with," he says of the old, sharp-tongued Brooks. "Now, I find myself more understanding of people's needs, more pa-tient than I was." Not that he's famous for giving out *kudos*, but he is toned down. If he reserves his accolades for only the select few, he keeps most of his barbs to himself. At worst, he may get worked up at a private party and do a sarcastic routine. For the press nowadays he is one-hundred percent cooperative. "With age," Brooks says, "you get to be a nicer person." This seems to be the only effect so far that age has had on Melvin. If he must get older, then he must, but there is no fear that he will really grow up.

But success has given him new insecurities, too.

Now, he stands to lose much more than when he had nothing. "He has to have his way," says a friend. Anyone who has ever worked with him will confirm that. "Now I have to worry about losing power, force, inspiration," he told Herbert Gold. But his doubts are under control. "I have targets, of course, to keep me going."

What does Brooks want out of life? Simple. He is after the biggest laugh ever laughed, just as he wants all the love there is, all the praise there is, all the attention, all the adulation, all of everything. But he is willing to work ceaselessly for it. He wants it—but he wants it *earned*. And he is willing to risk the best of himself for it.

Despite his unmatched reputation and earning power, Brooks's movies are still prepared on a step basis. He has an idea, writes a three-page treatment, and submits it to a studio. If they like it, they advance a small sum of development money. Brooks then expands his synopsis into a full-sized treatment. Once approved, more money changes hands, this time for the final script. This provides protection for Brooks, and limited risk for the studio. Few writers, even rich ones, can afford the year or more it takes to write a screenplay. The token advance pays the rent. It also serves to keep Brooks going. Writing can be a tedious labor. When you know someone has given you money, you have to deliver. The best way to stay alive as a good writer, according to Brooks, is to run a bulldozer through your conditioned values, learn to live frugally, which he hasn't, and take all the time you need to develop your ideas.

You also have to have enough strength and clout to resist the idiocies of the medium. Movies and television are so mechanized now that if a person has talent there are a lot of people in shiny suits waiting to grab him and chain him to a typewriter. A writer is expected to churn out scripts on demand. Pretty soon he's thinking the way the studio bosses are thinking. If he writes a scenario, he must consider not his ideas but whether Freddie Prinze—or whomever else is that week's hot potato—can play the lead.

Brooks has resisted it all. All of his work is exceptionally individualistic, and now exceptionally profitable. He wants to keep directing films, even if some of the joy of learning has worn off. He believes he can still improve. As long as he has something more to achieve, Brooks is ready to try. The challenge is to keep it simple, keep it clear, and yet make it his own, stamp it with the unmistakable Mel Brooks signature. And he has the courage, whatever the result, to emblazon his name above the title of his creation in the grand Hollywood manner.

He couldn't deny his films if he wanted to. He worries about every detail, from camera angles, lights, actors, and pacing, to having to stop at a certain hour for the unions. He is super-protective of his creation and the special mood that he must sustain to get it on film. He sweats and cries and groans through every frame. On top of it all, the financial axe is always ready to fall. The film mustn't exceed budget. It must make a lot of money. These are the rules. Brooks hears a small ghostly voice whispering to him from the back of every set, "Another dollar and you're out, kid."

As defiant as he is against the financial heads who run the film world and subsequently the world of Mel Brooks, he is also a realist. One of his goals is to be rich. And by any standard he's succeeded, though he's still confused about the exact amount. He still worries about whether to travel first or second class and whether to trade in his Buick Riviera with a dented fender for a new car. Despite a lingering poverty mentality, Brooks supports all the members of his family in style. "Funny is money!" he shouts. Then adds, "All I want is enough not to be oppressed by it." His real concern for profits is a matter of his own survival as an artist. Hollywood mathematics is pure and simple: More profits equals more artistic freedom. "If I could get the same control over my films that a novelist has over the written page or the artist over the canvas," Brooks says, "I'd be a happy man."

He is very nearly at that point. With two big hits in a row, Brooks has all the control that his nerves can handle. Howard Rothberg, Brooks's agent, a well-dressed young man who wears wide-lapelled suits and a Mickey Mouse watch, is very proud of his client. "He has total creative control. They don't understand, but they know he does it well. He has final cut—the best deal in the industry. What other directors have it? Woody Allen, Peter Bogdanovich, Mike Nichols, Francis Coppola. He has total recall. He pays attention to every frame. He'll say: 'In that scene, the effects come three frames too soon.' His creative control goes all through the campaign—publicity, selling, advertising, the whole works."

Herbert Gold believes that Mel Brooks has learned the philosopher's truth: "The mystery of life is not a problem to be solved, but a reality to be experienced—or, in his case, to be worked over in yoks."

Today, Melvin is never very far away from

being serious, even when he is his silliest. While going through the insane editing for *Young Frankenstein*, mimicking sound effects for everything from a locomotive to a virgin's orgasm, he worked himself into a frenzied hysteria. "Born Ham," he shouts. "Love It." But when the session ended, he turned to the man in the control booth and shook his head. "How 'bout that," he said. "A grown man making silly noises while Jews are running through the streets of Baghdad with their hair on fire."

He has other loves. Besides sex and spaghetti, Brooks loves to read. Until he met Mel Tolkin, head writer on *Your Show of Shows*, Brooks hardly read at all. As a kid, he was always too nervous and energetic to sit down with a book. Tolkin, who Brooks describes as "a big, tall, skinny Jew with terribly worried eyes," was an enthusiast of Russian novels. He introduced Brooks to Tolstoy, Dostoievski, Turgenev, and Gogol. "I read Tolstoy and fainted," says Brooks.

Another friend, Bernard Wolfe, recalls that Brooks used to knock on his door on Fire Island at midnight to talk about Dostoievski. Brooks moved on to Stendhal, Proust, Kafka—plus a few Americans such as Melville and Thoreau. "I read *War and Peace* every couple of years. I *have* to," he says, "because he's tops in taps."

The Russian novelists made Brooks realize it's a bigger ball park than the Bilko show. From the moment he read them he felt he wanted to achieve more than Doc Simon and Abe Burrows. Brooks wants to be the American Molière, the new Aristophanes. "My God," he says, "I'd love to smash into the casket of Dostoievski, grab that bony hand, and scream at the remains, 'Well done, you goddam genius.' " But then he added, nearly in the same breath, "In the midst of everything else, you gotta remember that the Ritz Brothers were the funniest people who ever lived. Forget that and you're *finished*."

Brooks's "act" is balanced by hard work and home cooking. When a film is shooting, he's up at six in the morning, grabs a cup of coffee, and then goes at it like a buzz saw. "Mel throws his head in the air a hundred times a day," says a friend, "but it always lands on his neck."

Mel's office on the Fox lot is surrounded with turn-of-the-century ghostly streets from *Hello Dolly!* His room is filled with movie posters of Zero Mostel in *The Producers* and Cleavon Little, complete with badge and Gucci purse. There's also a poster of wild-haired Gene Wilder and wild-eyed Marty Feldman in *Young Frankenstein*, and a large photo of himself leading a horse. There is a piano, many back copies of *Variety*, clips of reviews, and a trail of three-by-five index cards spelling out the story of *Silent Movie*.

When he's not working on a script he works on his friends. He is an amateur doctor; he wants to make people well, including himself.

Brooks has always been a passionate moviegoer. Once a week he orders a sandwich, pays twenty dollars to rent a sixteen-mm copy of a film, and invites friends to join him in his studio office to share a golden oldie—W.C. Fields movies, *City Lights*, the best of John Huston, and the comedies of William Powell and Carole Lombard. His all-time favorites include *The Blue Angel*, Pietro Germi's *Seduced and Abandoned*, *Big Deal of Madonna Street*, *The African Queen*, *Grand Illusion*, and *Some Like It Hot*. "To me," says Brooks, "Bergman is like Freud. Others stand on his shoulders." Bergman is "a thousand miles ahead of the pack." Samuel Beckett is his favorite playwright.

Brooks still thinks occasionally of doing more acting. He's considering doing a movie with screenwriter-director Robert Towne, who wrote *Chinatown*. He would act in it along with Anne Bancroft. She, according to Brooks, would get top billing because she's prettier and a little taller than he is.

The social life of Brooks and Bancroft is limited to weekends, and usually not even then. During the week they stay at home, says Brooks, and eat Raisinettes. Since he mentioned the chocolate-covered raisins in *Blazing Saddles*, he has been the recipient of carloads of candy from the Raisinettes company. Queried on his passion for Raisinettes, he told Herbert Gold, "Chocolate isn't good for teeth? Teeth aren't good for chocolate, either."

Transplanted to California, does Brooks miss his New York life? "I miss haircuts in New York. I miss the one millimeter of rudeness. I miss the dog _ _ _ _ _. No, revise that—dog-doody. Walking. You get exercise, you've got to avoid big presents the doggies have laid out for you. That's better for family reading. Broken field running, a choice of muggers. I miss the Village. A New York waterbagel really tests your teeth. They call something bagels here, but even people with false teeth can eat them. But the coal is here in L.A. I'm a coal miner. I'm here. If I have my family and a few good friends and my work, what difference where I am?"

He is identified with his constant flow of mimicry, wisecracks, helpfulness, marital and medical advice ("you have a little sinusitis, right?"), offers of record albums, and boxes of Raisinettes. He is helpful and friendly to all, "I love your face! It's so pretty!" he shrieks for hello, and then his voice grows hoarse and very precise, "And I remain, your obedient Jew, Mel Brooks."

Brooks is still a streetfighter, but one who's used to winning now. If he still feels the prickishness of "loser" somewhere under his skin, he gives no sign. He has the winner's stance. He's cocky, flashy, tough. The blows that rain upon his head aren't painful anymore, only tickling. He is the Heavyweight Champion of Comedy, and he won't make the mistake of letting himself get out of shape. It's still roadwork every morning at six, with a wad of Trident gum in his mouth and a box of Raisinettes sticking out of his back pocket. He's the forever kid. He's involved. He's vulnerable. He's looking for the same involvement in his audience.

Does he really believe that making movies is any hedge against death? Well, yes and no. "If Einstein and Shaw couldn't beat it, I don't stand much of a chance." But while he's here, he'll be heard. You can't beat death, Brooks believes, but it's better to go out with some chalk marks on your slate than with an empty blackboard that shows no trace of human existence. Brooks comments: "Nietzsche whispers to you: 'Without audacity there is no greatness.' Freud whispers to you: 'Why must there be greatness?' That fight's still going on. And you don't understand either one, because they're both whispering in German."

Perhaps then, the old saw is correct; what separates man from beast is that man is the only animal that laughs. And man would be no exception without a few charmed souls like Mel Brooks to help him remember just how funny the world can be, even when it's not.

OTHER SELECTIONS
FROM PLAYBOY PRESS

I CAUGHT FLIES FOR HOWARD HUGHES  $1.95

RON KISTLER

The extraordinary lifestyle of the world's richest recluse is revealed by a personal aide who worked for Hughes for three years.

THE SECRET HAPPINESS OF
   MARILYN MONROE                          $1.95

JAMES E. DOUGHERTY

Marilyn's first husband talks about his teen-age bride, their life together, and the ambitions that tore them apart. Includes a bonus collection of rare, early photos.

JIMMY THE GREEK                           $1.95

BY HIMSELF

From sports to politics to marriage, he's the ultimate odds-maker. One of the most powerful and fascinating person-alities of our times tells a story packed with hilarious and revealing anecdotes, inside information and solid advice.

THE DARK SIDE OF CAMELOT        $1.75

NELSON THOMPSON

The Kennedys—Jack, Bobby and Teddy—revealed in uncensored portrait of their lives, their "connections," their women and their power.

## ORDER DIRECTLY FROM: